The Purchasing Chessboard

Christian Schuh
Robert Kromoser
Michael F. Strohmer
Ramón Romero Pérez
Alenka Triplat

The Purchasing Chessboard

64 Methods to Reduce Cost and Increase Value with Suppliers

Christian Schuh	Robert Kromoser	Michael F. Strohmer
A.T. Kearney Ges.m.b.H.	A.T. Kearney Ges.m.b.H.	A.T. Kearney Ges.m.b.H.
Trattnerhof 1	Trattnerhof 1	Trattnerhof 1
1010 Wien	1010 Wien	1010 Wien
Austria	Austria	Austria
christian.schuh@atkearney.com	robert.kromoser@atkearney.com	michael.strohmer@atkearney.com

Ramón Romero Pérez	Alenka Triplat
A.T. Kearney GmbH	A.T. Kearney Ges.m.b.H.
Charlottenstrasse 57	Trattnerhof 1
10117 Berlin	1010 Wien
Germany	Austria
ramon.romero@atkearney.com	alenka.triplat@atkearney.com

Original German edition published by Gabler 2008.

ISBN 978-3-540-88724-9   e-ISBN 978-3-540-88725-6

DOI 10.1007/978-3-540-88725-6

Library of Congress Control Number: 2008940149

© 2009 Springer-Verlag Berlin Heidelberg

This work is subject to copyright. All rights are reserved, whether the whole or part of the material is concerned, specifically the rights of translation, reprinting, reuse of illustrations, recitation, broadcasting, reproduction on microfilm or in any other way, and storage in data banks. Duplication of this publication or parts thereof is permitted only under the provisions of the German Copyright Law of September 9, 1965, in its current version, and permissions for use must always be obtained from Springer-Verlag. Violations are liable for prosecution under the German Copyright Law.

The use of general descriptive names, registered names, trademarks, etc. in this publication does not imply, even in the absence of a specific statement, that such names are exempt from the relevant protective laws and regulations and therefore free for general use.

Cover design: WMXDesign GmbH, Heidelberg, Germany

Printed on acid-free paper

9 8 7 6 5 4 3 2   SPIN 12649488

springer.com

"Our success as consultants will depend upon the essential rightness of the advice we give and our capacity for convincing those in authority that it is good."

Andrew Thomas Kearney
(1892-1962)

Preface

The basic idea for this book was conceived in December 2005. At the time, various models for structuring sourcing strategies could be found in the literature. As different as many of these models were, they all restricted themselves to describing the content of sourcing strategies. What we felt was lacking was a tie-in between sourcing strategies and the specific situations confronting business enterprises. After experimenting with structures classified by industry, position in the product lifecycle, or concentration on the supplier market, we finally hit on the simplest structure of all: supply power versus demand power. What worked in the bazaars of Babylon, raised trading powers like Venice to greatness and formed the basis of the British Empire is still valid today!

The two axes of supply power and demand power offer an ideal approach for structuring sourcing strategies and classifying them in a logical manner. By January 2006, we had already isolated some 60 markedly different sourcing strategies and sorted them between the two axes. To provide a clearer visual distinction, we colored the fields in alternating colors in a chessboard pattern. Initial tests in coordination with clients in Austria, Germany and the USA proved highly promising. The logic of supply power versus demand power seemed to dovetail with the thinking adopted by executives themselves, and facilitated the tie-in between purchasing issues and corporate strategy.

Since then, we have further refined our Purchasing Chessboard™ and tested it extensively. It has also been applied in practice by clients in Australia, Austria, China, the Czech Republic, Finland, France, Germany, Italy, Russia, Slovenia, Spain, the UK, Ukraine and the US. The relevant sectors included automotive manufacturing and supply, military equipment (tanks), construction equipment, packaging, steel, transportation, foodstuffs, pharmaceuticals, energy utilities, telecommunications and banking.

This book has a highly ambitious goal: providing a comprehensive strategy for tackling any and all challenges in the field of purchasing. To this end, we have drawn on the collective experience and insights of A.T. Kearney. In the last three years alone, A.T. Kearney has carried out over 500 purchasing projects, involving the market placement of more than 500 billion dollars in spend. Despite the most sophisticated knowledge-management systems, we have found that face-to-face contact is still indispensable for exchanging information. Of all the colleagues who gave us valuable assistance as discussion partners in the writing of this book, we would like to particularly thank the following: Íñigo Aranzabal (Madrid), Thorsten Barkmann (Düsseldorf), Jan Fokke van den Bosch (Amsterdam), Dirk Buchta (Dubai), Stephen Fowles (London), Patrick Dolisie (Paris), Stephen Easton (London), Joachim Ebert (Chicago), Jules Goffre (Munich), Martin Haubensak (Düsseldorf), Kurt Hoch (Vienna), Günter Jordan (Munich), Theo Klein (Düsseldorf), Ruslan Korsh (Moscow), Robert Kremlicka (Vienna), Rick Kozole (Detroit), Lian Hoon Lim (Hong Kong), Dietrich Neumann (Berlin), Jean Dominique Rey (Paris), Thomas Rings (Munich), F. Nikolaus Soellner (Düsseldorf), Oliver Scheel (Düsseldorf), Sieghart Scheiter (Düsseldorf), Peter Wessmann (Düsseldorf) and Andrej Vizjak (Ljubljana/Munich). Our gratitude also goes out to our editorial team, especially Marianne Denk-Helmold, without whom this book would not have been possible.

Preface

We are confident that we have created a work that will be equally useful to all those involved in business purchasing – from the CEO to the staff in the field. We hope it will stimulate our readers to make real and effective improvements in their purchasing procedures. Enjoy!

Christian Schuh
Robert Kromoser
Michael F. Strohmer
Ramón Romero Pérez
Alenka Triplat

Table of Contents

Preface VII

1 **Purchasing: between a rock and a hard place?** 1

1.1 Survey results: the state of purchasing in industry 2

    Purchasing in industry 3

    Information systems support effective purchasing 3

    Targeted external communication with suppliers 4

    Demand and capacity planning must be observed 5

    Adequate involvement in strategic issues 5

    Tailored strategies for each sourcing category need to be strengthened 5

    Inadequate staffing 6

    Analytical deficits 6

1.2 A paradigm shift in purchasing 7

    Increasing concentration on the supplier market 7

    Rising energy prices 8

    Hunger for resources on the part of emerging economies 8

2		**From four basic strategies to 64 methods**	11
	2.1	Manage spend	15
		Demand management	16
		Co-sourcing	17
		Volume bundling	18
		Commercial data mining	19
	2.2	Change nature of demand	20
		Risk management	20
		Innovation breakthrough	21
		Technical data mining	22
		Re-specification	23
	2.3	Leverage competition among suppliers	24
		Globalization	25
		Tendering	26
		Target pricing	27
		Supplier pricing review	28
	2.4	Seek joint advantage with supplier	29
		Integrated operations planning	29
		Value chain management	31
		Cost partnership	32
		Value partnership	32
3		**Using the Purchasing Chessboard™**	35
	3.1	A company's fingerprint on the Purchasing Chessboard™	38
	3.2	Example of applying the Purchasing Chessboard™	41

	4	**The Purchasing Chessboard™.. 55**
A1		Demand reduction 57
A2		Compliance management... 59
A3		Procurement outsourcing 62
A4		Sourcing community... 65
A5		Bottleneck management 68
A6		Vertical integration 71
A7		Core cost analysis 73
A8		Invention on demand 75
B1		Contract management.. 80
B2		Closed loop spend management 82
B3		Mega supplier strategy 84
B4		Buying consortia 86
B5		Political framework management... 87
B6		Intelligent deal structure... 89
B7		Design for sourcing 91
B8		Leverage innovation network 93

C1	Bundling across product lines	96
C2	Supplier consolidation	98
C3	Master data management	99
C4	Cost data mining	102
C5	Product benchmark	104
C6	Composite benchmark	106
C7	Product teardown	110
C8	Functionality assessment	111
D1	Bundling across sites	114
D2	Bundling across generations	116
D3	Spend transparency	117
D4	Standardization	120
D5	Complexity reduction	122
D6	Process benchmark	125
D7	Design for manufacture	127
D8	Specification assessment	129
E1	Global sourcing	131

E2	Make or buy	134
E3	Supplier market intelligence	136
E4	RFI/RFP process	139
E5	Visible process organization (VPO)	144
E6	Collaborative capacity management	149
E7	Supplier tiering	151
E8	Value chain reconfiguration	154
F1	LCC sourcing	156
F2	Best shoring	160
F3	Reverse auctions	163
F4	Expressive bidding	165
F5	Vendor managed inventory (VMI)	166
F6	Virtual inventory management	169
F7	Sustainability management	170
F8	Revenue sharing	173
G1	Cost based price modeling	174
G2	Cost regression analysis	176

G3	Price benchmark	180
G4	Total cost of ownership	181
G5	Supplier development	184
G6	Total lifecycle concept	187
G7	Project based partnership	190
G8	Profit sharing	191
H1	Linear performance pricing	193
H2	Factor cost analysis	194
H3	Unbundled prices	195
H4	Leverage market imbalances	197
H5	Supplier fitness program	198
H6	Collaborative cost reduction	201
H7	Value based sourcing	203
H8	Strategic alliance	205

5	Closing Remarks	209
Appendix		211
About the authors		213

1 Purchasing: between a rock and a hard place?

The point of departure for this book was a perceived change in mood on the purchasing front. In our many talks with purchasing managers and senior executives, we increasingly gained the impression that a paradigm shift was in progress. Purchasing strategies that were successfully used for decades are no longer working. Suppliers are unilaterally increasing prices but are unwilling or unable to accompany higher prices with a guarantee of supply security. Buyers are in fear of losing face within their companies. Accustomed profit margins are collapsing.

Our first step was to analytically underpin these perceptions by taking stock of purchasing throughout industry. The methodological framework for our survey was provided by the "seven factors for success in purchasing" as defined by the observations of A.T. Kearney:

1. Purchasing must be an interdisciplinary, top-management task. The purchasing department must hold an equal rank alongside sales, R&D and production in the formulation and implementation of corporate strategy.

2. External communication must be a key element in purchasing. The company must speak to suppliers with one voice.

3. The purchasing department must work with analytical tools and strive to be better informed than suppliers. The traditional "arm wrestling" between purchasing and suppliers is therefore no longer necessary.

4. Based on the company's demand power and the suppliers' supply power, purchasing must develop a tailored strategy for each sourcing category in order to cut costs and add value.

5. Purchasing must be integrated seamlessly, directly and equally alongside sales and production when it comes to demand and capacity planning.

6. Purchasing must have appropriate information systems at its disposal, and be able to ascertain at any time "who buys what from which supplier."

7. Purchasing must be staffed with a sufficient number of technically and commercially competent personnel, and must be seen as a desirable career stage within the company.

1.1 Survey results: the state of purchasing in industry

As part of the purchasing survey, 600 CEOs of industrial companies were asked to rate the degree to which the "seven factors for success in purchasing" were being applied at their firms. Of these 600 CEOs, 200 responded. The companies surveyed were active in automotive supply, mechanical engineering, foodstuffs, pharmaceuticals, transportation, raw material processing and energy grid operations.

At over 30 percent, the response rate was well above the average for surveys of this kind. This already provides a clear indication of the importance accorded to purchasing by top-management today.

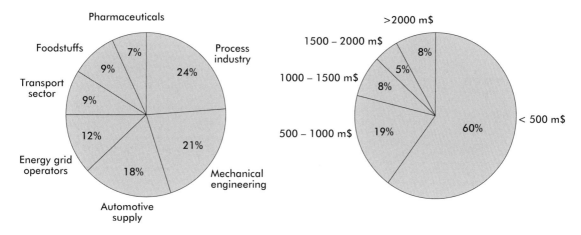

Fig. 1. Segmentation of participants by industry and revenue size

(The letter we sent out asking each company to participate was addressed to the CEO or Managing Director.)

Purchasing in industry

The arithmetical mean of all the responses from companies suggests that their purchasing departments are already highly developed. The range of possible responses was as follows: "1 – Not true," "2 – Partially true," "3 – Mostly true," "4 – Completely true."

Information systems support effective purchasing

With 3.3 out of a possible 4.0 points, the question about appropriate information systems produced the highest concurrence. Today's companies, many of which have grown through acquisitions, produce a variety of

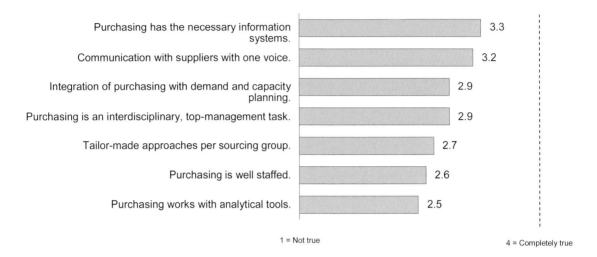

Fig. 2. Respondent's rating of their company's purchasing

similar and/or different products at a large number of locations, supported by frequently differing IT systems. Therefore, purchasing needs a consistent and highly integrated IT system that enables transparency over purchases across the organization and answers the question "Who buys what from which supplier?". Top-managers unanimously gave their existing information systems a positive rating.

Targeted external communication with suppliers

With 3.2 out of a possible 4.0 points, the question about targeted external communication with suppliers also produced a high level of concurrence. In the worst case, purchasing is confronted with the situation where a supplier has already been pre-determined, for example, by specifying a customized product. On the whole, industry is in good shape as far as targeted supplier communication is concerned; it manages to avoid twin-track strategies that can be exploited by savvy sales people from the supplier's side.

Demand and capacity planning must be observed

With 2.9 out of a possible 4.0 points, the integration of purchasing in demand and capacity planning was generally rated as good. Reconciling anticipated customer demand with capacities available from the company's own production facilities and from suppliers requires a rolling planning process, one in which sales, production and purchasing must all be assigned equal weight.

Adequate involvement in strategic issues

With 2.9 out of a possible 4.0 points, purchasing is widely perceived as an interdisciplinary, top-management task. Most of the cost structure of products and services is determined during the early phases of strategic planning. In order to give purchasing a formative role in this context, it must be included as an equal partner alongside sales, R&D and production in the formulation and implementation of corporate strategy.

Tailored strategies for each sourcing category need to be strengthened

With 2.7 out of a possible 4.0 points, the use of tailored cost-cutting/value-adding strategies was given a medium-to-low rating. Depending on the demand power of the company and the supply power of the suppliers, highly differentiated strategies are needed. And yet consulting experience has shown that purchasing often works with just a handful of similar strategies, such as volume bundling or long-term contracts. This leaves a great deal of untapped cost-savings/added value, and also harbors the risk of unduly close ties to monopolistic suppliers.

Inadequate staffing

With 2.6 out of a possible 4.0 points, the question of purchasing staff received the second-lowest level of concurrence. Purchasing can only participate equally in strategic planning, produce substantiated analyses or develop differentiated strategies for cutting costs and increasing value if it can draw on a sufficient number of highly qualified, technically and business savvy employees. As reported in the media, companies are currently finding it difficult to hire qualified candidates. Moreover, purchasing is not yet perceived as an attractive career stage at many companies, so that internal recruitment channels have not been very successful either.

Analytical deficits

With 2.5 out of a possible 4.0 points, the ability of purchasing to use analytical tools was given the poorest rating in the survey. Modern purchasing combines technical and commercial information with knowledge of the supply markets and is therefore well prepared for negotiations with suppliers. The goal is to know more about the subject matter of the negotiations than the supplier does. However, we can still find buyers in many companies who view negotiations primarily as a psychological game and use this approach to conceal knowledge deficits on their own part.

1 Purchasing: between a rock and a hard place?

1.2 A paradigm shift in purchasing

Our survey of purchasing in industry showed that decision makers were increasingly uneasy with the strategies, analytical capabilities and human resources in place at their purchasing departments. How should we explain this?

Ever since the 1980s, today's generation of purchasing executives has been accustomed to operating on a predominantly buyer's market with falling material costs. In the past, relatively simple methods such as tendering, bundling volume and concluding multi-year contracts enabled purchasing to obtain price cuts from suppliers of between one to three percent per annum. This "golden age" of purchasing is now over, however, and we find ourselves at the start of a seller's market. There are three main reasons for this:

- Increasing concentration on the supplier market.
- Rising energy prices.
- Hunger for resources on the part of emerging economies.

Increasing concentration on the supplier market

The cost pressure that could be consistently exerted in a buyer's market only intensified the already existing trend towards concentration. To be able to use economies of scale and thus cope with cost pressure, suppliers were increasingly forced to consolidate via merger and acquisition. Especially those suppliers who were passing on their full productivity gains to customers (at the expense of their own profitability) frequently found themselves taken over by competitors. From this point of view, buyers can be said to have been a bit too successful. As a result, the supply power of the remaining suppliers has risen dramatically compared to previous years.

Rising energy prices

For many years, the rise in energy prices was ignored as a temporary anomaly or explained away as the result of extraordinary circumstances (e.g. tension in the Middle East). By now, however, the debate on sustainability and global warming, along with the growing shortage of fossil fuels, has made it clear that high energy prices are here to stay. Some forecasts even predict an oil price as high as 200 dollars per barrel. On the other hand, agile companies can exploit high energy prices for their own benefit, for instance by supporting technological innovations to solve the crisis. Nonetheless, most suppliers simply use price increases as an argument for raising their own profits.

Hunger for resources on the part of emerging economies

Along with concentration on the supplier market and surging energy prices, the demand for resources by rapidly growing economies such as Brazil, China, India (and in future, Russia) is one of the main drivers of changing background conditions. We are already seeing developments inconceivable only a few years ago. For instance, steel is becoming scarce, while Europe is thinking once again about investing in coal production. Meanwhile, Africa, with its abundant deposits of raw materials, suddenly finds itself once again at the center of foreign ambitions.

As a result of these three factors, buyers are confronted with suppliers who calmly demand price increases of five percent and more, yet are still unable or unwilling to guarantee the necessary supply security.

The simple techniques that used to be so effective on the buyer's market of previous decades (e.g. tenders, bundling volume and concluding multi-year contracts) are largely useless against these new forces. Thus, many companies already find themselves "between a rock and a hard place" in terms of purchasing. As our survey of purchasing in industry has shown (see above), this fact has not gone unnoticed by top-management.

2 From four basic strategies to 64 methods

To help purchasing meet the new challenges of the seller's market, A.T. Kearney has developed the Purchasing Chessboard™. This represents the condensed experience and insights acquired by A.T. Kearney from over 500 purchasing projects carried out all over the world during the last three years (in which a spend of over 500 billion dollars was placed on the market), as well as from thousands of similar projects conducted over the last three decades. The Purchasing Chessboard™ has the goal of assisting buyers in all kinds of relations with suppliers. Its basic concept derives from the relationship between supply and demand.

Clearly, supply and demand are two economic forces that have helped determine the rise and fall of dominant civilizations throughout history. The bazaars of ancient Babylon, the Roman Empire, Venice in its heyday, the British Empire, the emerging world power of the USA the unification of Europe via the Coal and Steel Community, the EEC and the EU – all these historical developments were steered to a great extent by the laws of economic supply and demand. There is no reason to believe that these laws are less relevant today than they were in preceding millennia, or that this is likely to change in the foreseeable future.

Using supply power and demand power as the fundamental methodological concept to categorize supply relations in purchasing has the advantage of being immediately comprehensible to all departments and managerial levels of a company. Since the managing board and/or top-management are especially prone to think in these categories, it becomes easier for purchasing to mesh its own ideas with the overall corporate strategy.

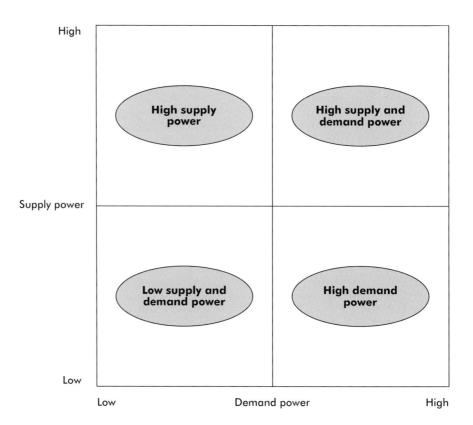

Fig. 3. The purchasing playing field

2 From four basic strategies to 64 methods

So how can supply power and demand power be turned into a methodology for "hands-on" purchasing? The answer lies in a portfolio that covers the gamut from low-to-high supply power, as well as from low-to-high demand power.

Let us first use four fundamentally different situations to illustrate such a portfolio:

- **High demand power:** A big carmaker (e.g. Volkswagen) buys forged parts. There must be hundreds, if not thousands, of forged-part manufacturers throughout the world, and out of these there must be at least several dozen who are qualified to meet Volkswagen's quality and volume requirements. In this case, Volkswagen is a buyer in a position of overwhelming power vis-à-vis its forgings suppliers, and is able to exploit competition amongst its suppliers to its own advantage.

- **High supply and demand power:** If the same big carmaker now wishes to buy engine management systems from Bosch, the situation is completely different. In many segments, Bosch holds a *de facto* monopoly. Nevertheless, Bosch is just as dependent on the big carmakers as they are on Bosch. In this case, securing joint, long-term advantages is unquestionably in the interest of both parties.

- **High supply power:** Even the demand power of a big carmaker has its limits, especially when oligopolistic market conditions prevail. A good example is the purchasing of energy, such as electricity and natural gas. While Volkswagen certainly purchases a very large quantity of energy, it is largely dependent upon the inelastic production and distribution structures in Europe. Companies confronted by high supply power will consistently strive to bring about fundamental change in the nature of the demand in order to free themselves from the control of the supplier.

- **Low supply and demand power:** An example of low demand power on the part of a big carmaker is air travel. The situation is more balanced than in the preceding example, however, since deregulation of the airline market has actually produced results. Along with negotiating discounts, a key question to ask in this context is whether traveling by plane is necessary or whether it could be avoided altogether. Thus, the company is largely able to steer its own demand.

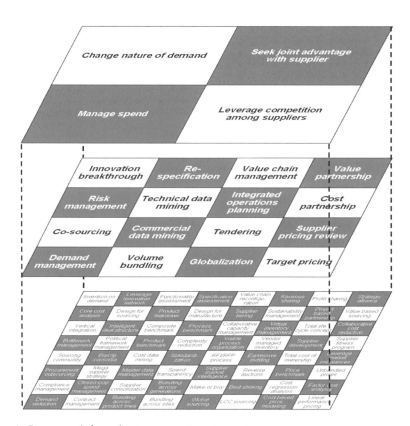

Fig. 4. Framework for selecting sourcing strategies

2 From four basic strategies to 64 methods

The portfolio of demand power and supply power can be broken down into almost any number of fields. A.T. Kearney has introduced three structuring levels (see Fig. 4):

- 4 fields – Basic strategies designed to specifically support discussions between the company's purchasing department and top-management.

- 16 fields – Approaches that are extremely useful in interdisciplinary discussions (e.g. with the R&D department).

- 64 fields – Methods that form the actual chessboard and provide an operating tool for use by purchasing.

In the following section, the three levels of the Purchasing Chessboard™ are outlined. A detailed description of the 64 methods with case studies can be found in Chapter 3.

2.1 Manage spend

In the case of low supply and demand power, the first basic strategy involves professional steering of demand. Manage spend first of all requires detailed knowledge of who is buying what from which supplier. Based on this, one can then consider the possibility of offsetting low demand power by bundling demand, either within the company or across company boundaries. These considerations should be backed by an uncompromising analysis of whether the demand in question is actually justified. The approaches for cutting costs and adding value within this basic strategy are demand management, co-sourcing, volume bundling and commercial data mining. These approaches and their underlying methods are briefly described below.

Demand management

Demand management achieves savings by reducing a company's demand from selected suppliers and taking full advantage of optimized contracts. Demand management encompasses the following strategies. (Here and in the following chapters, these are designated "A1" to "H8," just like the fields of a chessboard; as an aid, the Purchasing Chessboard™ at the end of the book can be unfolded.)

A1 **Demand reduction:** Objective analysis of the justification for a particular demand. (E.g., is it really necessary for someone to fly or could air travel be replaced by video conferencing?)

A2 **Compliance management:** This primarily involves the increased use of master agreements and preferred suppliers, as well as compliance with company wide policies (e.g. travel policy).

B1 **Contract management:** Even the best contracts are of little use if nobody is familiar with them. Contract management has the aim of creating transparency with regard to existing contracts throughout the company, as well as consolidating contracts, thus achieving better terms for all internal customers.

B2 **Closed loop spend management:** The aim of this holistic approach is to permanently observe all areas of potential value leakage (e.g. unutilized payment terms) and take appropriate measures when required.

Co-sourcing

Co-sourcing is an approach that can be used when a single company does not represent any significant demand power in the market of a particular sourcing category and suffers disadvantages as a result. In co-sourcing, demand is pooled across sourcing categories or with other companies. Co-sourcing encompasses the following methods:

A3 **Procurement outsourcing:** Responsibility for purchasing is delegated to an outsourcing partner with significantly greater demand power.

A4 **Sourcing community:** Several companies, each with low demand power join forces in order to achieve sustained savings. Sourcing communities go beyond mere volume bundling arrangements: they are able to pursue complex strategies because they can share resources, e.g. analysts or infrastructure, with the other members of the sourcing community.

B3 **Mega supplier strategy:** Its primary aim is to make both the company and the supplier aware of how large the mutual business actually is. Instead of negotiating on the level of individual sourcing categories (for which the company has little demand power), all purchases from the same supplier are negotiated together.

B4 **Buying consortia:** Buying consortia are loose cooperations of firms aimed at obtaining advantages on the sourcing market. In contrast to sourcing communities, they are of limited duration (i.e. until the end of the respective project).

Volume bundling

Volume bundling is one of the traditional purchasing approaches, whereby savings are achieved through realization of benefits from economies of scale on supplier's side. Although this approach is well known, one often forgets how much a company using it can realize by receiving supplier's concessions. Especially in the case of high fixed cost products or those requiring long set-up times, the scale effects can be considerable: e.g., if fixed cost accounts for 30 percent, doubling the volume should make price reductions of 15 percent possible. Volume bundling encompasses the following methods:

C1 **Bundling across product lines:** Bundling similar bought-in parts for all product lines, e.g. a white goods manufacturer consolidates sourcing of all electric motors.

C2 **Supplier consolidation:** Bundling similar bought-in parts from one competitive supplier and cutting out the others. This specifically means eliminating smaller suppliers and strengthening ties to bigger or strategically important ones.

D1 **Bundling across sites:** Bundling across individual company locations can be used specifically for those sourcing categories that could be supplied by the same supplier on global or regional markets.

D2 **Bundling across generations:** Bundling across product generations is especially important for project-driven businesses. Concessions are obtained from the supplier for the current project on the basis of binding or non-binding promises for the subsequent generation.

Commercial data mining

If our company only knew what we already know! There is enormous potential hidden in accumulated commercial data – often slumbering in SAP or Oracle systems. With the aid of targeted sorting and intelligent analyses, it is possible to create transparency, identify potential through standardization and enable rapid realization of cost savings. The use of commercial data encompasses the following methods:

C3 **Master data management:** Classification of all material/supplier master data through the application of standardized logic, consistent link-up of master data to the ordering system and avoidance of loosely worded purchase orders.

C4 **Cost data mining:** In this case, existing data on a sourcing category is analyzed in depth in order to identify any savings potential. For instance, this may include comparing the discount rates within a corporate group.

D3 **Spend transparency:** Creating transparency for all spending within the company in the form of a spend cube. The main axes of the cube are sourcing categories, suppliers and sites, which can be sliced and diced across all dimensions.

D4 **Standardization:** Replacement of custom specifications by standardized parts and industrial standards.

2.2 Change nature of demand

In cases where supply power is high, the second basic strategy is to change the nature of the demand. High supply power exists in cases whenever a supplier succeeds in establishing a monopolistic or oligopolistic position thanks to a unique technical advantage or exclusive market access. Quite often, a market constellation of this kind is not inevitable but is in fact brought about, either knowingly or unknowingly, by the buying company itself. Changing the nature of demand requires sounding out the limits – i.e. determining to what extent technical specifications can be modified so as to regain freedom of choice. Experience has taught that nearly all monopolies can be circumvented. The remaining residual risk can then be managed through the use of appropriate measures.

The approaches for cutting costs and adding value within this basic strategy are risk management, innovation breakthrough, technical data mining, and re-specification. These approaches and their underlying methods are briefly described below.

Risk management

The term "risk management" is used to designate the sum of defensive measures that can be employed in order to ensure that the customers can be supplied and that the company's financial outcomes remain plannable. Risk management encompasses the following methods:

 Bottleneck management: A combination of steps to facilitate proactive avoidance, early recognition and adoption of timely countermeasures against bottlenecks. The aim is to ensure the supply of end products to the customer under all circumstances.

A6 **Vertical integration:** In a seller's market with constantly rising prices and restricted supply, the long-spurned method of vertical integration is coming back into favor.

B5 **Political framework management:** With skillful lobbying, it is possible to maneuver a monopolistically operating supplier into a position that works to the advantage of the dependent company.

B6 **Intelligent deal structure:** Especially when purchasing from monopolistic suppliers, careful drafting of contracts is of paramount importance. Contracts skillfully designed to suit the specific demand structure of the company can be a competitive factor of considerable importance.

Innovation breakthrough

Whether as a result of monopolies or patents, or because specifications are excessively geared to a single supplier, companies sometimes find themselves in a position of complete dependence. In cases of this kind, the only solution is an innovation breakthrough that will fundamentally change the rules of the game. Innovation breakthrough encompasses the following methods:

A7 **Core cost analysis:** In essence, core cost analysis is a "zero-based method" to product development. Instead of dragging along all the extras that have attached themselves to a product over the years, one goes back to basics and asks what functions are absolutely essential. The product is then radically optimized in line with these basic requirements.

A8 **Invention on demand:** Patent-protected suppliers constitute a particularly difficult challenge to purchasing. Under the invention on demand strategy, which is based on the TRIZ method, alternative technical solutions are systematically developed, taking account of ideas from all scientific fields.

B7 **Design for sourcing:** By fostering closer cooperation between R&D and purchasing, design for sourcing generalizes specifications to such an extent that they are no longer tailored to suit just one particular supplier.

B8 **Leverage innovation network:** R&D is fostered through cooperation in a cross-company innovation network. This also allows the company to gain new insights into innovative technologies. By looking beyond its own backyard, the company frees itself from long-standing supply dependencies.

Technical data mining

Increasing differentiation, shorter product lifecycles and growing product variety make sourcing increasingly complex. As a result, it is also becoming more difficult to practice volume bundling or to achieve economies of scale from suppliers. The first step, therefore, is to apply the appropriate tools to bring order into the apparent chaos. By using analysis and benchmarking, it should be possible to identify potential improvements that can be realized in a joint effort between R&D and production. Technical data mining encompasses the following methods:

C5 **Product benchmark:** Product benchmarking enables the comparison of the different design solutions that are available on the market.

C6 **Composite benchmark:** In this case, a selection of competing products is sent to several suppliers for component analysis. The suppliers make proposals and submit offers at both the component and product level. By combining the best proposals, a "best of the best" concept is arrived at, while insight is also acquired into the suppliers' production costs.

D5 **Complexity reduction:** Product complexity is rendered visible and tangible through structured variant trees. As a result, the number of variants can be systematically reduced.

D6 **Process benchmark:** Process benchmarking is the comparison of costs for individual production steps, such as surface treatment of turned parts. The resulting figures provide a basis on which purchasing can negotiate processing costs directly with the supplier.

Re-specification

Many of the costs of a product are already determined in the early phases of its development. If one cannot reduce cost within the scope of existing specifications, there is only one thing to do: go back to the drawing board! The obstacle in this case is to get the creative process going again. After all, there was good reason why the product was designed the way it was. Thus, the key question is, "Do I really need a particular feature or characteristic for my product to be successful on the market or to be able to produce it efficiently?" Re-specification encompasses the following methods:

C7 **Product teardown:** Product teardown means breaking down competitors' products into their component parts and comparing them with one's own solution.

C8 **Functionality assessment:** The costs which each function of a product incurs are attributed to that function. An interdisciplinary team then identifies functions that are dispensable or that could be provided more cheaply.

D7 **Design for manufacture:** Design for manufacture is a systematic process for designing products (or modifying their design) so that they are easy and inexpensive to produce.

D8 **Specification assessment:** Specification assessment means critically evaluating current specifications and asking whether they are in fact useful or merely increase cost and complexity. Specifications that are not necessary are amended accordingly.

2.3 Leverage competition among suppliers

Where high demand power exists, the third basic strategy is to leverage competition among suppliers to the advantage of the company. Variations of this basic strategy are further fueling competition through appropriate measures on the supplier market, or influencing supplier pricing through analytical tools.

The approaches for cutting costs and increasing value within this basic strategy are globalization, tendering, target pricing, and supplier pricing review. These approaches and their underlying methods are briefly described below.

Globalization

Globalization opens up possibilities not just on the selling side, but especially on the purchasing side. With the opening of markets in Eastern Europe, China and India, over a billion additional workers have become available globally; workers whose low factor costs are being increasingly paired with the highest levels of skill. However, utilizing the globalization lever means taking advantage not just of low-cost countries, but of the worldwide supplier market as well.

Globalization encompasses the following methods:

E1 **Global sourcing:** Global sourcing aims at selecting the most competitive suppliers worldwide. This may sound obvious, but it is still true today that European companies mostly use European suppliers and US companies mostly use US ones, whereby this ignominious list could be continued almost indefinitely.

E2 **Make or buy**: Except where core skills are concerned, internal production must be exposed to competition with the supplier market, and vice versa. Focusing attention on this topic often produces surprising results.

F1 **LCC sourcing:** Low-cost country sourcing is primarily aimed at identifying, assessing, and utilizing suppliers from countries with low factor costs.

F2 **Best shoring:** Best shoring aims at evaluating what region and what supplier are particularly suited for outsourcing within the value-creation process. Along with a business case analysis, this strategy also involves holistic assessment of risks.

Tendering

Probably the most commonly used approach is tendering. Although the effectiveness of tendering has declined since the end of the buyer's market (at least for the time being), it would be a mistake to dismiss this approach. Tendering is a particularly effective way of obtaining transparency regarding prices on the supplier market. Successful use of this approach requires expertise regarding the various steps of the tendering process, including identification of potential suppliers, preparation and mailing of the tender documents, analysis of bids, and negotiations with suitable suppliers. The practice of tendering encompasses the following methods:

E3 **Supplier market intelligence:** Supplier market intelligence comprises the systematic gathering, evaluation, and utilization of information on all incumbent and potential new suppliers.

E4 **RFI/RFP process:** The RFI/RFP process encompasses the systematic preparation, dispatch, and evaluation of supplier information (RFI = request for information) and solicitations for offers (RFP = request for proposal).

F3 **Reverse auctions:** Through the use of web-based tools, reverse auctions can be used to accelerate the negotiating phase of the tendering process.

F4 **Expressive bidding:** Expressive bidding refers to obtaining supplier offers while allowing for "if-then" conditions (e.g. delivery period, service levels).

2 From four basic strategies to 64 methods

Target pricing

Since only very few suppliers are prepared to disclose their cost structures, the use of the target pricing lever will require alternative ways of determining cost structures. Depending on the initial situation, methods of varying analytical depth can be used to ascertain target prices. Some of these methods call for expertise in statistics. Target pricing encompasses the following methods:

G1 **Cost based price modeling:** Cost based price modeling is a process-oriented method for determining target prices. The bases for target prices are the individual process steps, to which reference values can be applied.

G2 **Cost regression analysis:** Cost regression analysis is a statistical method for determining target prices on the basis of several technical parameters.

H1 **Linear performance pricing:** Linear performance pricing is a method for identifying the main technical cost driver for the product price of a group of materials.

H2 **Factor cost analysis:** Factor cost analysis is a method for systematically identifying, analyzing, and comparing relevant factor costs. It can be used as the basis for comparing the factor costs of various suppliers and thus determining target prices.

Supplier pricing review

Quite often, the prices of existing suppliers are not systematically calculated on the basis of "cost-plus" logic. Development or tooling costs are usually factored in inconsistently, and mixed costing robs pricing of its transparency. Supplier pricing review introduces uniform standards for pricing. Supplier pricing review encompasses the following methods:

G3 **Price benchmark:** Price benchmark is a method of comprehensive comparison of product prices and contract terms.

G4 **Total cost of ownership:** This concept comprises the holistic identification, evaluation, and analysis of non-recurring costs, production costs, transport costs, complexity costs, and operating costs.

H3 **Unbundled prices:** Unbundled prices aim at breaking down the total price of a product or service into the relevant cost elements (e.g. component vs. system costs, production vs. development costs), in order to invite separate bids for each of these elements during a tendering process.

H4 **Leverage market imbalances:** In this method, the aim is to systematically identify market imbalances and exploit them for purchasing purposes. Market imbalances can come about as a result of variable capacity utilization across certain regions, differing price mechanisms, or fluctuations in factor costs.

2.4 Seek joint advantage with supplier

Where there is both high supply power and high demand power, the fourth basic strategy aims at searching jointly with the supplier for advantages. The different variants of this basic strategy depend on the scope and intensity of the partnership. The scope can range from coordinated demand and capacity planning to complete intermeshing of the value chain. Meanwhile, the intensity can range from project based sharing of costs to the sharing of financial success and risk.

The approaches for cutting costs and increasing value within this basic strategy are integrated operations planning, value chain management, cost partnership, and value partnership. These approaches and their underlying methods are briefly described below.

Integrated operations planning

Rather than achieving direct reductions in a component price, integrated operations planning tries to achieve targeted savings by decreasing inventories and making sales forecasts more reliable which in turn improves the capacity and demand balance. The supplier and customer collaborate in a spirit of trust and exchange information with one another, often supported by internet applications. This is a true partnership on the operating level, but one that calls for great openness in terms of exchanging information. It is an important approach not only for cutting costs but also for adding value, since it avoids component/capacity bottlenecks, thus increasing sales revenues. Integrated operations planning encompasses the following methods:

E5 **Visible process organization:** This is an innovative form of organization characterized by the permanent co-location of decision makers and the implementation of a dynamic re-planning process. Through improved information flows, the company avoids disruption costs.

E6 **Collaborative capacity management:** Deficient communication between customer and supplier can lead to capacity bottlenecks and production losses, with sometimes serious consequences. Collaborative capacity management ensures ongoing reconciliation between demand and capacity with regard to a selected critical component volume.

F5 **Vendor managed inventory:** Here, inventory management is placed entirely in the hands of the supplier. The supplier usually has electronic access to consumption and inventory data. Greater planning freedom enables the supplier to cut costs.

F6 **Virtual inventory management:** All inventories at the supplier and customer locations, as well as in the hands of logistics partners (i.e. en route), are included in the inventory optimization process. If IT inventory systems do not supply integrated data, an auxiliary solution will be necessary.

Value chain management

The focus of this approach is on systematically optimizing the value chain and the associated value-generating units. Trustworthy handling of company data (sales revenue, value stages, suppliers' buying costs, etc.) is a fundamental requirement for the successful implementation of improvements through value chain management. Value chain management encompasses the following methods:

E7 **Supplier tiering:** Supplier tiering can work in two directions: it uses key suppliers to bundle upstream tier-2 suppliers, thus relieves the company of the need to manage a large number of suppliers; or it does the exact opposite by breaking up already existing structures and cutting out tier-1 supplier.

E8 **Value chain reconfiguration:** Existing value chains are analyzed, broken down into their component parts, and then recombined in a new configuration. The aim is to acquire or maintain maximum control of key stages and processes, thus internalizing core competencies as a competitive advantage.

F7 **Sustainability management:** Sustainability management is the integrated management of the company and its value-creation chain in accordance with economic, social, and ecological principles. For example, environmental measures may enable the company to save costs or prevent damage to its image.

F8 **Revenue sharing:** A defined percentage of sales revenue is shared with the supplier. This makes sense especially in cases where a bought-in part contributes significantly to the overall perception of a product.

Cost partnership

Here the goal is to optimize costs through collaboration on a partnership basis. Crucial for the success of this approach is a focus on a small number of suppliers and on achieving genuinely significant savings. A cost partnership encompasses the following methods:

G5 **Supplier development:** Supplier development has the aim of fostering attractive new suppliers and/or small incumbent ones, and developing them into key suppliers.

G6 **Total lifecycle concept:** The total lifecycle concept regulates in detail how sales revenue and costs are distributed between the company and suppliers over the entire product lifecycle.

H5 **Supplier fitness program:** The supplier fitness program helps suppliers through targeted measures to eliminate weaknesses within their own value creation processes, thus making them more competitive.

H6 **Collaborative cost reduction:** The company and suppliers jointly develop ideas for cutting costs and then share the savings.

Value partnership

The goal of a value partnership is to optimize value growth and to share the business risk. Crucial for the success of this approach is the creation of a genuine win-win situation. A value partnership encompasses the following methods:

2 From four basic strategies to 64 methods

G7 **Project based partnership:** For companies and suppliers wanting to cooperate for a limited period and within a limited scope, a project based partnership is a suitable cooperation model.

G8 **Profit sharing:** Instead of the traditional method of paying suppliers a product-based purchasing price, one can agree to share the profit. This especially makes sense when the supplier has an overwhelming influence on the success of the business.

H7 **Value based sourcing:** Value based sourcing is an approach whereby suppliers are selected in terms of their capabilities and are continually encouraged to innovate, the goal being value maximization.

H8 **Strategic alliance:** Strategic alliances with suppliers, i.e. permanent collaboration with a partner, are appropriate where a company does not wish or is not able to maintain certain strategic capabilities internally, or has no possibility of vertical integration.

An average buyer may have simple methods such as tendering, volume bundling, and multi-year contracts at his fingertips. An outstanding and highly experienced buyer, on the other hand, can draw upon 10 to 15 different methods for cutting costs and increasing value with regard to suppliers. However, as this book shows, there are no less than 64 independent methods of this type! To work hands-on with the 64 methods, we recommend to always keep an eye on the Purchasing Chessboard™ at the end of the book which can be folded out for this purpose. Continual visualization of the Purchasing Chessboard™ will ensure that purchasing makes full use of all the tools available. The individual fields and methods of the Purchasing Chessboard™ are described in detail in Chapter 3. First, however, we will explain how to use the Purchasing Chessboard™.

3 Using the Purchasing Chessboard™

The Purchasing Chessboard™ is used to assign strategies and methods for cutting costs and increasing value to specific sourcing volumes. The first step is to find an appropriate classification for a given sourcing volume. For example, if a steel producer is planning to invest in a new coking plant, there are (roughly speaking) three levels on which an order can be placed:

- Plant – The entire coking plant is contracted out to a single turnkey supplier.

- Process plant – The coking plant is divided into the coking plant proper and the gas treatment section, with contracts concluded separately for each part.

- Components – The coking plant is broken down into the coke-oven batteries, coal preparation and screening, oven machinery, chimneys, coal tower, and quenching towers, with contracts placed separately for each.

Note that there is no right or wrong in this case. The choice of the appropriate structure largely depends on the capabilities existing within the company.

It is generally advisable to consider several strategies simultaneously so as to weigh the pros and cons of bundling or separation with the greatest possible transparency.

The second step is to map the sourcing volumes on the Purchasing Chessboard™. When positioning elements of spend along the demand power axis, one must consider the following:

- What share of the relevant sales market (of a region) does the company have?
- What growth perspectives does the company offer suppliers?
- What competency-enhancing possibilities does the company offer suppliers?
- How can suppliers improve their image by working for the company?

A company has high demand power when suppliers are not able to circumvent it, when the company is the biggest buyer of certain products (and is experiencing strong growth), when the company collaborates regularly with suppliers on innovations, or when the company has a strong reputation.

When positioning elements of spend along the supply power axis, one needs to consider the following:

- How many credible suppliers are there?
- What market share do these suppliers hold?
- What are the M & A dynamics on the supplier market?

- How easy is it for new suppliers to enter the market?
- How easy is it to change suppliers?
- What is the availability of substitution products?
- How easy is it to switch to substitution products?
- What is product availability; are there signs of future bottlenecks?

High supply power exists when suppliers are able to operate on the market as monopolists, when their products are protected by patents, when barriers to new entrants and substitution products are high, and when demand exceeds supply.

Once sourcing volumes have been positioned on the Purchasing Chessboard™, one must conduct a plausibility check. A cross-comparison of the sourcing volumes' positions is particularly useful for this purpose.

After the plausibility check is complete, one can begin to work profitably with the Purchasing Chessboard™. For each sourcing volume, one first identifies the basic strategies, approaches, and methods located around its position on the Purchasing Chessboard™. Positioning on the Purchasing Chessboard™ does not identify any single method with mathematical accuracy, but rather suggests a group of adjacent/related methods. We will now discuss how to best apply these various methods to a given sourcing volume.

3.1 A company's fingerprint on the Purchasing Chessboard™

Just as no fingerprint is identical to any other, applying the Purchasing Chessboard™ to the procurement portfolio of a company produces a unique profile – the fingerprint of the company, as it were. To illustrate this specificity, here are six selected examples:

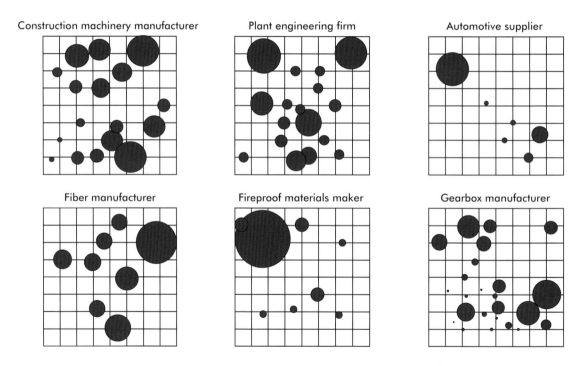

Fig. 5. Examples of applying the Purchasing Chessboard™

In each example, categories are represented by circles. The diameter of the circle is proportionate to the spend of the category. A category with a spend of 100 million dollars per annum is therefore represented by a circle whose diameter is twice that of a circle representing a spend of 50 million dollars per annum. The categories are positioned on the Purchasing Chessboard™ following the steps described above.

Looking at these six fingerprints, the first thing that catches the eye is the different number of categories per company. While the automotive supplier manages with only six categories, other companies (e.g. the gearbox manufacturer) differentiate among over 20 categories. The reason for the variable number of categories lies mainly in the nature of the respective business. For example, the automotive supplier makes stampings. In line with this focused business, the automotive supplier distinguishes only a small number of categories on the Purchasing Chessboard™. The construction equipment maker, on the other hand, offers a broad product portfolio, from small aerial work platforms to gigantic hydraulic excavators. Thus, the differing nature of these businesses is physically reflected on the Purchasing Chessboard™.

Another factor apparent when looking at our six examples is the different weighting of the categories. This weighting is also derived from the nature of the line of business. In the case of the automotive supplier, steel accounts for over 70 percent of the company's spend. Steel is therefore the dominant category in the company. Similarly, raw materials are a dominant category for the maker of refractories. For the fiber producer, pulp is in fact the biggest sourcing category, but in contrast to the prior examples it is not dominant. In the case of the construction equipment manufacturer, the EPC (engineering, procurement and construction) company and the gearbox maker, each has a number of large categories alongside several smaller groups, producing an altogether balanced picture.

Another interesting aspect is the distribution of categories on the Purchasing Chessboard™. Both for the gearbox manufacturer and the fiber producer, more than 50 percent of the spend is located in the right half of the Purchasing Chessboard™. That means these companies have the advantage of relatively high demand power with regard to the bulk of their spend. In the case of the automotive supplier and the refractory maker, by contrast, most of the spend is clearly located in the region of low demand power. For the construction equipment maker and the EPC company, the spend is relatively evenly distributed in terms of demand power. When it comes to supply power however, only the gearbox maker has the predominant share of its sourcing volume in the favorable area (i.e. low power on the part of suppliers). In the case of the construction equipment maker, the EPC firm, and the fiber producer, there is a tendency for spend to be located in the high supply power range. The situation of the automotive supplier and the refractory maker is particularly unfavorable, since the predominant share of their spend is located in the area of high supply power.

Just as the six companies have variable fingerprints on the Purchasing Chessboard™ with regard to their categories, they also differ in terms of their purchasing focus. In the case of the automotive supplier and the refractory maker, purchasing has a clear emphasis: ensuring lots of supply security while also being able to cushion market fluctuations. Suppliers that enjoy such high supply power, paired with low demand power on the part of customers, tend to exploit their position. Production capacities are allocated by the supplier according to optimization of profits. In such situations, supply bottlenecks accompanied by price rises are virtually the norm.

For the construction equipment maker, the EPC company and the fiber producer, the situation is very different. While all three also have some categories in similarly unfavorable positions as in the prior example, most of their categories lie where high demand power meets high supply power. In these companies, purchasing will seek to establish genuine win-win situations with suppliers. At the gearbox maker, the situation is different again. While we once more find the two constellations described before (though in less pronounced form), we also see purchasing concentrated in the area where high demand power is paired with low power on the part of suppliers. Thus, purchasing can still successfully play the traditional role of price cutter.

3.2 Example of applying the Purchasing Chessboard™

We will now use the construction equipment maker to illustrate how the Purchasing Chessboard™ can be successfully applied in practice.

This example can then be applied by analogy to the other five firms discussed above. We will begin by fleshing out our real-life scenario with more detail. Our construction equipment maker manufactures a broad range of products, from small aerial work platforms to gigantic hydraulic excavators at dozens of plants in North America, Europe and Asia at revenues well above eight billion dollars.

The construction equipment maker's suppliers are responsible for a considerable part of value creation, and spend accounts for over 60 percent of revenues. The company distinguishes between 17 main categories, which are positioned on the Purchasing Chessboard™ as shown in figure 6:

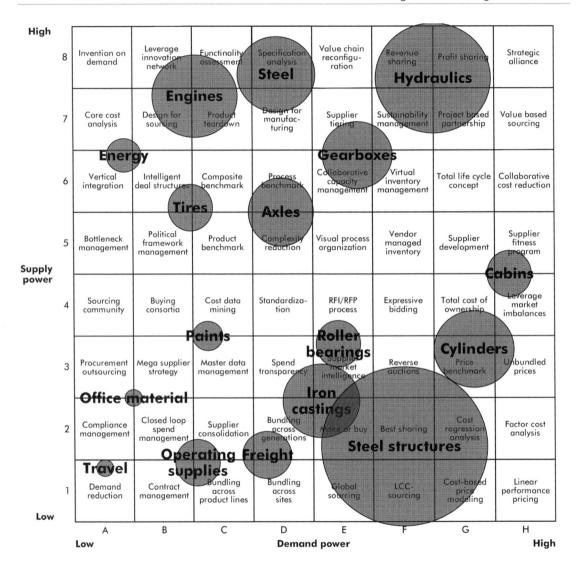

Fig. 6. Purchasing Chessboard™ for a construction equipment maker

A.T. Kearney was asked to carry out an extensive purchasing project over a period of several years for this particular construction equipment maker. Before the project, purchasing in the company was handled relatively autonomously by the various divisions and plants. Collaboration across divisional and regional boundaries sometimes took place on a case-by-case basis, but was always restricted to particular initiatives driven by highly motivated individuals. The purchasing project had the goal of applying the Purchasing Chessboard™ in order to achieve a substantial and sustained reduction in material costs, and to make savings sustainable by establishing a group-wide purchasing organization.

In five of the 17 categories, the construction equipment maker had relatively low demand power. These five categories were also associated with low power on the part of the suppliers. The five groups in question were freight, MRO, paint, office material, and travel:

- Freight: Looked at globally, the company's demand power in the area of freight was on the low side. Supply power on the hotly contested market for freight and logistics was also very low. The only option was to optimize freight routes while optimizing price, which represented the biggest lever. The methods effective in this regard were bundling across sites and expressive bidding. The latter gave suppliers the chance to submit offers for routes containing "if-then" conditions (e.g. a further reduction in the price per mile if the supplier is also used on other routes).

- MRO: This category comprised many different maintenance, repair and operation supplies. The construction equipment manufacturer's low demand power in this area was again matched by equally low strength on the supply side. Thus, the effective methods were supplier consolidation and demand reduction. Of particular interest in this context was the use of "vending machines" similar to those for selling soft drinks. Authorized staff members were furnished with chip cards that they could use at their own discretion for purchasing materials. The mere fact that consumption could be individually recorded resulted in substantial reduction in demand.

- Paint: Paints and coatings were critical products because they had to comply with numerous standards, especially in terms of durability or exposure to extreme weather conditions. Thus, the company's production system was geared to the paint suppliers. Compared to automobile and commercial vehicle producers, even such a big manufacturer of construction equipment had little demand power. But the suppliers had little supply power as well, as there were a considerable number of producers able to provide the required paints and coatings. However, an obstacle to switching suppliers was the need for time-consuming tests. Thus, the best methods for use in this area were RFI/RFP process and standardization.

- Office material: In this category, the suppliers had very little supply power. There were a large number of different firms offering office material, so there was considerable competition. At the same time, the demand power of the construction equipment manufacturer (and practically all other companies) was also low. The appropriate lever, therefore, was consolidating and analyzing the company's own needs, creating transparency, bundling the company's demand, and automating the purchasing process through the use of e-catalogs, which also led to simplified billing. The best methods in this case were bundling across sites and supplier consolidation (e.g. use of one supplier at the regional, national or even international level).

- Travel: Supply power was low because suppliers, such as small travel agencies and large global operators, were in fierce competition with one another. (The same kind of cutthroat competition also occurs among car rental firms and airlines.) But demand power was also low since, depending on the company, there was little demand for travel in the construction machinery industry. Thus, consolidation and analysis of global demand brought little in the way of savings. The best methods here were spend transparency (which many travel agencies offer through the analysis of credit card payments), paired with demand reduction and compliance management. The latter meant defining precisely, in the case of airline and other tickets, what class of travel could be booked for which business trip.

In five of the 17 categories, the construction equipment manufacturer had relatively low demand power, against high power on the part of suppliers. The five groups in question were engines, steel, axles, tires, and energy:

- Engines: As far as engines were concerned, construction equipment manufacturers had very weak demand; truck makers bought a much greater volume of engines for example. At the same time, supply power was extremely high, so that it could be difficult to obtain engines at all. Moreover, they were extremely critical sourcing items, since new emission control regulations required engines to be replaced by certain dates. Also, many construction machines were designed around the engine, so that changing suppliers within one generation was hardly realistic. One of the methods applicable in this case was design for sourcing (i.e. for the new generation). However, it had to be done in such a way that any engine could be used. Through detailed assessment of the functionalities, one had to provide the option of leaving out as many special engine components as possible, making life easier for the engine manufacturer. All special features would then be added by the construction equipment manufacturer itself.

- Steel: First, we should distinguish between high-strength steel and standard steel. In the case of high-strength steel, the construction equipment manufacturer competed directly with the defense industry. The latter was less price-sensitive, and with its heavy demand repeatedly caused capacity bottlenecks at suppliers for certain processes (e.g. heat treatment). In the case of standard steel, effective methods had proven to be specification analysis, (i.e. determining what qualities are actually needed) and supplier tiering. One eye-opener was that the construction machinery manufacturer bought just as much steel as BMW! However, the steel was normally purchased in small quantities by individual sites through so-called service centers. A new approach used in this context was board room-to-board room discussions with the big steel producers, whereby risk management proved an effective way to improve planning certainty with regard to steel prices.

- Axles: Demand power was moderate, since construction equipment manufacturers bought far fewer axles than, say, commercial vehicle/truck manufacturers. The axles were designed to go with a special chassis, and were more or less customized products outside of serial production. The axle suppliers themselves had moderate supply power, as there were numerous axle producers. Capacity and competence were already being developed in China and India, e.g. by a rapidly growing industry. Important methods applicable here were complexity reduction and process benchmark.

- Tires: As with engines, tires were characterized by bottlenecks, since the suppliers were so stretched that they were reluctant to produce the special types needed for construction equipment and, to some extent, farm machinery. There were even instances where finished units left the assembly lines without tires. It was therefore of crucial importance to conclude agreements with the tire manufacturers to produce the quantities needed if the construction equipment manufacturer was to grow. At the same time, a search was made for suppliers prepared to invest in developing new products, so as to provide the company with more alternatives. A crucial method was finding an intelligent deal structure that integrated investment in a supplier's production line as a way to ensure supply security. Another method was product benchmark of competitors' products to determine whether other types of tires could be used (e.g. ones filled with plastic foam, as offered by several suppliers, instead of air-filled tires). In order to take timely countermeasures against bottlenecks, the company pursued bottleneck management.

- Energy: Because of the shortcomings in attempts to liberalize the energy market, there was little to be done in this area. Appropriate on-site measures at plants were able to prevent demand peaks, thus slightly reducing electricity bills. The relevant strategy, therefore, was to achieve intelligent deal structures, while attempting to conclude contracts during optimal market phases. This could involve choosing one-year, two-year or three-year contracts, based on the prevailing situation on the energy market.

In five of the 17 categories, the construction equipment manufacturer had relatively high demand power, against moderate supply power on the part of the suppliers. The five categories in question were steel fabrications, castings, cylinders, cabs, and bearings:

- Steel fabrications: Structurally, construction equipment consists primarily of steel. Most of the structural steel work, which did not require any exceptional skills (except for shaping and welding high-strength steel), had long been outsourced to suppliers. The construction equipment maker was one of the biggest and most highly rated companies in the industry. This represented a highly attractive package for suppliers and thus demand power was very high. In all key economic regions of the world, there were a large number of suppliers able to produce steel fabrications for construction equipment manufacturers. New suppliers could be relatively easily qualified, and quality defects were easy to detect (i.e. they did not require any highly sophisticated inspection/testing equipment), so that switching suppliers was also easy. The supply power of the suppliers was very low overall. In the project, the supplier landscape was found to be quite varied. North America predominantly used North American suppliers and one internal supplier from Mexico; Europe used a mix of Western and Eastern European suppliers; Asia used mostly local suppliers. The main methods from the Purchasing Chessboard™ were best shoring and low-cost country (LCC) sourcing. Especially at the start of the project, cost regression analyses were important for identifying high-price oases and setting the corresponding focuses. Of special interest were new transport methods that secured just-in-time delivery, even from distant suppliers. The solutions chosen were consignment stocks and, in one case, the transport of welded assemblies in the weight category of 10 to 15 metric tons from China to Germany via the Trans-Siberian Railway.

- Castings: Here, the situation was basically similar to that for steel fabrications. One of the main differences was that spend was significantly smaller. The construction equipment industry also competed more intensely with other industries for iron castings than for steel fabrications. The demand power of the construction equipment maker was therefore rated as average. While there were numerous suppliers of iron castings worldwide, many had to be ruled out because of the size and weight of most components. As in the case of iron castings, quality problems such as cavities or sinkholes often only came to light in the course of subsequent processing. Thus, switching suppliers was not as easy as with steel structures. The supply power of the suppliers was rated as moderate. In the course of the project, attempts were made to put together attractive packages for certain categories of iron castings. This was done especially through bundling across sites and utilization of the RFI/RFP process.

- Cylinders: While steel structures dominate the design of construction machines, hydraulic cylinders are essentially the component that enables them to work. Almost every time heavy loads have to be lifted or moved, or stones have to be quarried or broken, hydraulic cylinders are at work. Because of their size and their need for isolation against damage and dirt, hydraulic cylinders for construction machines constitute a highly specialized market. Thus, suppliers supplying this market tended to have only one construction equipment maker as a customer. One of the dominant players on this market therefore had a very high demand power.

If a supplier met the requirements of the construction equipment maker and was able to supply the corresponding sizes, that supplier could be very quickly introduced for a class of products. This meant that the supply power of the suppliers was only moderate. Exceptions to this rule were suppliers producing exceptionally long or heavy cylinders; these suppliers had succeeded in attaining quasi-monopoly status.

Especially at first, the project used the methods of price benchmarking, unbundling of prices, and cost regression analysis. Cylinders were broken down into their component parts (tubes, rods, valves, etc.). This created price transparency which led to a first wave of savings with existing suppliers. In a second wave, suppliers from markets with low factor costs, especially Asia, were introduced. This enabled further substantial savings to be made.

- Cabs: Driver's and operator's cabins are mainly found in construction machines although, broadly speaking, the cabins of farm machinery and local utility machines are also similar. For the makers of cabins, there is no getting past the construction equipment makers. A large, prospering construction equipment maker with corresponding development potential is naturally even more attractive. Demand power was therefore rated as very high. As the cabin formed the interface between the machine and the person who spends all day working in it, the cabin was of overriding importance in building a brand image. A manufacturer would not casually put the look and feel of a construction machine at risk by changing the supplier. As part of the project, a total cost of ownership method was applied to identify which cabin type and configuration had the greatest marketing success at the lowest cost. Additionally, supplier development and supplier fitness programs were used to help a number of suppliers to update their production processes. In the first year, the resulting savings were shared; in the second, they all went to the construction equipment maker.

- Bearings: Depending on the type of bearings, demand power varied widely. While small, standard roller bearings were relatively easy to source in many countries, capacities still needed to be built in China and India (but would eventually offer a good basis for global sourcing). Slewing rings with diameters of several meters were sometimes subject to bottlenecks or had long delivery times (i.e. supplies were generally unreliable). An important method in this case was make or buy (i.e. possible in-house production of these critical slewing rings).

In the remaining two of the 17 sourcing categories, the construction equipment maker had relatively high demand power, against high power on the part of suppliers; these two product groups were hydraulics and gearboxes:

- Hydraulics: Roughly speaking, the hydraulics of a construction machine consist of the following components:

    - Pumps, which are coupled directly to the construction machine's diesel engine and provide pressure for the hydraulic system.

    - Valves and manifolds that regulate and transmit the pressure to actuators.

    - Actuators – essentially hydraulic motors with the previously discussed hydraulic cylinders.

    - Hoses that connect the foregoing components with one another.

The main applications for mobile hydraulic systems are construction machines. A leading construction equipment maker therefore has high demand power. A large part of the know-how that goes into construction machines involves hydraulics. There are only a small number of suppliers able to configure hydraulic systems. Construction equipment makers who put their faith in suppliers on account of their hydraulics expertise therefore create suppliers with very high supply power. During the project, the construction equipment maker laid the foundation stone for its own worldwide hydraulic competence center. Instead of having the basic hydraulics developed at dozens of different sites and being in a position of automatic inferiority vis-à-vis the supplier, the construction equipment maker wanted to develop enough know-how to be able to build complete hydraulic systems itself. This would then enable components from different suppliers to be combined much more freely than before. Until this approach took effect, the company pursued project based partnerships and strategic alliances to achieve win-win situations with hydraulics suppliers.

- Gearboxes: One can distinguish between two basic areas of application for gearboxes: gearboxes in the drive train, and gearboxes for all other features on the construction machines. The project focused on the second type (i.e. gearboxes e.g. for winches). The supply power of the suppliers of these gearboxes was very high, because there were only a limited number able to meet the special requirements of construction machines. On the other hand, the demand power of construction equipment makers was also considerable, since they were the main customer group for this kind of gearbox. On the established markets, there were few new suppliers. In Asia, especially India and China, capacities were growing rapidly. Thus, the main methods employed were collaborative capacity management and project based partnerships.

In conclusion, through consistent application of the Purchasing Chessboard™, the construction equipment maker managed to achieve dramatic cuts in material costs on the order of dozens of million dollars. And this in a market environment that was extremely unfavorable for many of the categories and that was characterized by generally rising prices.

3 Using the Purchasing Chessboard™

The positive experience of the construction equipment maker is only one of a large number of success stories for A.T. Kearney clients in a wide range of industries. Thus, it is evident that systematic use of the Purchasing Chessboard™ can continue to produce benefits even in a seller's market.

4 The Purchasing Chessboard™

This chapter is intended as a reference for users. The 64 methods contained in the Purchasing Chessboard™ are explained in detail and illustrated by examples. For easier navigation, the individual methods are arranged as on a competition chessboard, from A1 to H8:

Fig. 7. The Purchasing Chessboard™

As a further aid, the Purchasing Chessboard™ shown here is repeated in a foldout version at the end of this book.

A1 Demand reduction

What would it be like to not have to buy anything at all? In the 21st century, certain groups of indirect material can be simply eliminated. A paperless office is now feasible since all work can be done via computer and all correspondence conducted via SAP and email. In light of current advances and in the face of rising energy prices, it is conceivable to have a company where none of the personnel have to travel because they are able to conference with colleagues and customers at the other end of the world in a virtual meeting room that feels almost true-to-life.

These are just some of the ideas behind the concept of reducing demand as a way of cutting back or eliminating certain purchased products. Appropriate strategies can be found in many areas. By adopting a systematic and well-communicated procedure, for example, a company can save energy costs with no detriment whatsoever to either its personnel or processes (e.g. switching computers off instead of leaving them on stand-by overnight, or turning the heating down by one degree or the air conditioning up by one degree). Office supplies (paper, pens, etc.) also tend to be viewed by employees as items they can appropriate for their own private use. There are a number of simple systems available for monitoring the issuance of supplies that normally do not need any follow-up. The mere fact that the company knows what supplies an individual is removing generates increased discipline in use. The core elements of demand reduction are as follows:

- Establishing cost awareness and corresponding standards.
- Improving and streamlining approval processes.
- Making increased use of lower-cost substitution products.

- Reducing the frequency of use.
- Limiting the scope of requirements.
- Reducing purchased quantities.
- Eliminating the demand for certain products.

These core elements are most effective when used in tandem, but even the application of just a few will result in savings. As a savings mentality does not match the corporate culture at some companies, consistent change management is a success factor that should not be ignored. In this case, it is necessary to explain the broader context and spell out why the measures are meaningful and what alternatives exist.

Case example: Reduction in travel costs at an IT company

As part of a cost-reduction scheme, an IT industry company analyzed its travel costs. The following questions were asked: What are the reasons for business trips? Are they internally or externally based? What factors influence the choice of hotel and flight?

A team studied the needs and routines of the personnel. Proceeding on this basis, a number of steps were identified for reducing demand, ranging from "soft" measures to influence employee awareness to highly aggressive measures for eliminating demand altogether. Here are some examples:

- Raising cost awareness through internal communication of examples. Facts were provided showing how much more expensive a flight can be if booked less than 14 days before the travel date.

> - Greater emphasis was given to the use of video conferencing as a substitute for travel.
>
> - Especially in internal discussions and training events, attempts were made to reduce the frequency of personal meetings so as to directly eliminate demand.
>
> - An approval process was introduced for all travel.
>
> This program enabled demand to be reduced by between 10 and 20 percent, depending on the department. It also sharply raised the employees' cost awareness.

A2 Compliance management

What use are carefully negotiated contracts and the resulting savings if product users within the company do not order from the corresponding suppliers? Either because of inadequate transparency, badly defined responsibilities or simply due to a lack of incentives, framework purchasing agreements often remain unutilized. Instead, preference is given to relationships with local suppliers.

Compliance management has the purpose of clearing up messes of this kind, especially through the detailed documentation of purchasing outside the selected supplier circle.

A key component of the control process is careful documentation of deviations from the rule in the form of non-compliance reports. These reports must be completed by the product user as part of the ordering process whenever he or she wishes to source from a supplier not included in the preferred circle. Non-compliance may be permitted in the following cases, for instance:

- Business needs that can generally not be covered by the scope of products and services of the selected suppliers.

- Specific (short-term) demand that the selected suppliers are not able to supply at the time in question.

Initially, deviations of up to ten percent are tolerated, with only bigger deviations triggering a reaction. After a certain time, the margin can be reduced to three or even zero percent. In order to achieve complete compliance with the contracts and agreements concluded by the company, a number of conditions must be fulfilled:

- The preferred suppliers selected by purchasing must be clearly communicated within the company; product users have to know what agreements exist and who the preferred suppliers are.

- The ordering process must be structured in such a way as to prevent inadvertent non-compliance (e.g. by allowing certain product users to place orders with the selected circle of suppliers only). The catalog of products that can be ordered from these suppliers is individually restricted. This is frequently done in the case of office articles, for example.

- The processes must be user-friendly so that users comply voluntarily and not because the "bureaucracy" forces them to do so.

- Guideline compliance must be supported by positive (and also negative) incentives, both for the product user and the purchaser, whose work is naturally oriented to the needs of his/her internal customer.

Ultimately, it is up to the top-management to set an example by adhering to the rules and by insisting on compliance.

> *Case example: Bundling agency work volumes at a chemical company*
>
> A chemical company was forced to tackle the issue of compliance after it was discovered that over 70 temporary staffing agencies (suppliers) were providing personnel to just a single site. This was due to long-standing relationships with some of these suppliers, though in some cases the ties were too close.
>
> The key question was how to ensure that the company's internal users of staffing agencies would no longer hire personnel at their own discretion but rather obtain them from the cheaper suppliers specified by purchasing. The board and divisional managers were involved in order to restructure the ordering process. The solution was to deploy purchasing and HR as a service center between the internal users of temporary staff and the staffing agencies. Thus, internal users are now no longer able to hire directly from the personnel firm of their choice, but have to notify the service center of their staffing requirements. The service center then selects appropriate personnel from specified suppliers.
>
> The crucial success factor for this strategy is to ensure that the quality of the agency personnel meets the expectations of the internal users. In the end, 50 of 70 personnel agencies could be eliminated at the aforementioned site alone. The annual savings from just this one measure amounted to several million US dollars.

A3 Procurement outsourcing

We are seeing increased outsourcing not just of call centers and wage-accounting etc., but also of activities that more directly affect a company's value generation process. Thus, purchasing has now also found its place on the outsourcing market. Before the step towards outsourcing purchasing is taken, two core questions must be answered:

- What services are expected? Outsourcing partners offer companies the complete range of activities on the transaction side: ordering material, comparing invoices with orders, paying suppliers, making optimum use of contracts and spot buying, administration of (consignment) inventories, demand management, standardization and administration of master data, even including strategic issues such as definition of sourcing strategies and implementation of cost optimization.

- What material and service groups are suitable for contracting out to outsourcing partners? These specifically include materials and services used by a large number of companies across a wide range of industries. A classic example is operating materials and supplies. In the case of these items, purchasing usually has little price leverage due to the small quantities that need to be bought, while there are numerous suppliers and dealers on this highly competitive market. By bundling the volume for all of their clients, outsourcing partners are able to obtain significantly better terms from suppliers. At the same time, process costs are optimized, because it is no longer necessary to generate orders for very small quantities (i.e. the work is now done for several firms all at the same time).

Outsourcing of the purchasing function, or at least parts thereof, is prepared and implemented in four steps:

- The first step is to evaluate the options for outsourcing. The internal costs for the personnel in purchasing and the additional process costs for maintenance of data occurring outside of purchasing must be identified and compared with the costs of external providers of purchasing services. On the other side, the potential for minimizing the costs of purchasing under both options is determined. The internal potential should be based on historic figures, while the external potential is defined directly by the prospective supplier. (Because of bundling effects and the resulting significantly higher demand power, the external potential is usually higher.) A business case can then be generated to evaluate the feasibility of outsourcing. An outsourcing decision should require the approval of top-management.

- The next step is to define the outsourcing model. This includes preparation of a service agreement with targets, roles, and responsibilities as well as a description of the purchasing process.

- The purchasing process is then placed in the hands of the external provider. The material data, requirements, supplier information, and specifications for delivery are also handed over. During implementation, all contracts are newly concluded. In the case of companies with several sites, implementation normally takes place over a period of 12 to 18 months.

- Ongoing control of the external provider must then be put in place. A mechanism must be created that allows performance to be continuously measured and enables conflicts to be resolved as quickly as possible.

Through procurement outsourcing, the company is able to participate in the much greater demand power of an outsourcing partner with lower prices and lower process costs, and is also able to minimize its business risk. In addition, outsourcing enables purchasing to focus on strategic questions.

Besides a clear definition of the distribution of functions between internal and external services, another critical success factor for procurement outsourcing is a clear definition of the scope of services to be performed by the external provider.

Case example: Outsourcing of operating materials and supplies by an automaker

An automaker placed the purchasing of operating materials and supplies in the hands of an external provider. By bundling volumes with those of its other clients, the provider was able to obtain much more favorable prices and to offer 10 to 15 percent lower prices. By also entrusting inventory management to the provider, it was possible to reduce inventory costs by 40 to 60 percent. Similar savings were also achieved in the field of complexity reduction. As the outsourcing partner was already working for other companies with similar demand, it was possible to use 30 to 50 percent less material numbers through improved EDP systems and by matching suppliers' catalogs.

A4 Sourcing community

Several companies with low demand power can join forces in order to achieve savings. Many companies have opted to outsource the management of certain product groups, especially those not at the core of their value-creation process; this enables them to focus their purchasing resources on issues of strategic importance. In the case of sourcing communities, companies organize themselves within a formal structure, with the collaboration intended to last for a long time. If the collaboration is done properly, savings of 5 to 15 percent will generally be possible, rising to as much as 50 percent in special cases.

But sourcing communities can do more. Because they are able to share resources, e.g. analysts or infrastructure, they make it possible to pursue sophisticated strategies even for low-volume sourcing categories. The aims of sourcing communities are closely linked to the size of the companies involved:

- Smaller companies at the same location can make joint purchases of technical articles from one supplier, or achieve better terms for the supply of operating materials and supplies.

- Medium-sized firms in favorable sourcing regions can share the effort and expense of identifying and qualifying suppliers.

- Large companies can consolidate their demand for raw materials and have the materials bought on global markets by experts at the best terms.

In line with these widely differing goals, different types of sourcing communities can be identified:

- **Size of the participating companies**: Here, a distinction is made between cooperations involving partners of equal strength and those with a mix of small and big partners.

- **Geographical focus**: In this case, it is necessary to decide whether a geographical cluster should be formed or whether the sourcing community should be open to companies from various regions.

- **Sourcing category focus**: The cooperation may focus on only a few product groups, or it may cover virtually the entire demand of its members.

- **Roles and responsibilities:** A fundamental distinction must be made between sourcing communities whose activities are restricted to identifying suppliers (and perhaps negotiating master agreements), and those that also handle ordering on behalf of their members.

- **Interests and corporate strategies**: A study by A.T. Kearney has shown that 81 percent of companies form sourcing communities with partners from within their own industry.

The success of sourcing communities depends to a large extent on the choice of suitable partners. The partners should all pursue a similar business philosophy and have similar expectations regarding the collaboration. Since working together in a sourcing community means a major cultural change for many companies, strong backing by top-management is essential, especially at first. Also important is that the group be of manageable size. Although the underlying idea of a sourcing community is an aggregation of purchasing volumes, small organizations with only a small number of members have proved to be more agile and more effective. Attention should therefore be paid to exclusivity. Irrespective of the legal form of the sourcing community, it should be headed by a single individual.

This person should be impartial towards all the members of the sourcing community. He or she must ensure a balance of interests internally and communicate externally (towards the suppliers) with one voice. The definition of management rules (e.g. sourcing principles and decision-making guidelines) should therefore take place early in the process.

Case examples: Successful sourcing communities

There are numerous examples of successful sourcing communities. The following are just a few: The Technical Operating Marketing Company (TOMCOM) was formed by Bell Atlantic, Nynex, US West New Vector Group, and AirTouch Communications with the goal of improving purchasing of mobile handsets and other devices. For older cars, replacement parts and service work offered by the proprietary subsidiaries and authorized dealerships are often too expensive. As a result, a close network of independent service/repair shops and wholesale/retail firms has been established in Germany and other European countries. These companies are usually too small to buy the requisite broad range of spare parts and accessories at reasonable prices. Nonetheless, a broad range of products is vital for independent service and repair workshops, as they normally offer their services for all major automotive brands. Thus, many of these companies already joined forces decades ago in the form of sourcing communities, some of which also compete with one another.

The idea of sourcing communities has now also entered the public sector. For example, a few years ago Austria began to bundle the demand of all its ministries and subordinate government bodies via a single "Federal Procurement Agency."

Bottleneck management

It happens even in the best business relationships: sooner or later, a bottleneck occurs, no matter how long the company has been working with the same supplier, and no matter how closely the relevant departments at the two companies work together. A supply bottleneck can easily trigger hectic troubleshooting. The first thing to do, however, is to examine the situation in greater detail. What was the actual cause of the bottleneck? Was it just an unfortunate coincidence that caused production to break down? Or was there some systemic flaw that could reappear at any time?

In order to prevent future supply bottlenecks, the first step is the most important: namely to conduct a detailed analysis of the circumstances. When this is done, one quite often finds that the bottleneck affects only a few critical parts. The core of the future purchasing strategy should therefore aim at gaining as much freedom of action on the supplier market as possible.

Bottleneck management starts with three short-term measures:

- Establishing targeted program management and focusing resources on problem components.

- Near-term change of supplier (focusing on development and test resources for short-term approval).

- Dispatching a number of employees to the supplier; obtaining delivery forecasts from the supplier which can be updated daily; ensuring timely internal communication.

Over the medium term, more incisive measures are possible:

- Substituting parts or eliminating variants.

- Further supplier changes in order to achieve greater diversification.

- New developments and the use of new technologies in order to reduce dependence on old technology.

The three long-term recommendations for avoiding supply bottlenecks are:

- Building up additional suppliers with capabilities identical to those of current suppliers.

- Identifying suppliers who are not yet on the necessary level but that can be developed further with measures already in the drawer.

- Dual sourcing (i.e. using at least two suppliers in parallel for critical components).

Case example: Bottleneck management by a maker of mining equipment

A maker of mining equipment was highly dependent on a supplier of hydraulic systems. The dependency derived from the fact that the supplier had delivered excellent work over many years and had repeatedly presented innovative products that had helped the mining equipment maker become highly successful. The supplier therefore accounted for nearly two-thirds of the total procurement volume with regard to hydraulics.

Around the year 2000, the mining industry found itself in a severe downturn. With investors shifting to the internet, the "old economy" looked very old indeed. After two more lean years, the hydraulic supplier took a fateful decision. On the basis of forecasts that mining was entering a long phase of stagnation, production lines were amalgamated and replacement investments canceled. However, events took exactly the opposite turn from what the supplier had planned for. The investment boom in China and India triggered a surge in demand for raw materials that is still underway today. Mining firms started to invest in machinery on a large scale, and the maker of mining equipment was soon "bursting at the seams". Unfortunately, the supplier was not able to keep pace, so that bottlenecks were an almost daily occurrence. Huge half-finished excavators were blocking up the production shop, but could not be moved for lack of certain hydraulic components.

Once the extent of the problem had become clear, the mining equipment maker put a process of bottleneck management in place. This involved a detailed analysis of the situation with the goal of finding viable medium and long-term solutions. The analysis centered on the following questions:

- Precisely which parts are problematic and lead to bottlenecks in the sourcing process?

- What alternatives do other suppliers offer, and how long would it take to obtain their parts?

- What possibilities are there for substitution? Variant trees were drawn in order to identify substitution possibilities.

> As a result of this analysis, it emerged that only around 10 percent of the parts were genuinely problematic in terms of procurement. Consequently, the following solution was identified and pursued: As a short-term goal, the supplier was required to issue daily status reports, precisely specifying which parts would be delivered at what time. For some critical items, almost identical parts were available from some of the supplier's competitors. For these items, a change of supplier was implemented in only four weeks. Normally, a change of this kind takes over six months. This extraordinarily fast supplier change was achieved through a joint effort on the part of development, quality control, production, and purchasing. Over the medium term, items in which the supplier had a monopoly were replaced by simpler products that could be bought from several of the supplier's competitors. From a long-term perspective, the company management has entered into close collaboration with a new supplier, and this is being consistently built up and promoted as a counterweight to the existing supplier.

A6 Vertical integration

Originally driven by capital markets seeking to limit volume risks and reward a focus on core competencies, vertical integration has seen a general decline in the course of the last few decades. This strategy was underpinned by dependable suppliers, rising productivity and, as a result, constantly falling prices.

In the seller's market now in evidence, the pendulum is swinging back. Companies that still have access to raw materials through the last remnants of vertical integration find themselves better placed to compete on the marketplace than their trimmed-down rivals. Consequently, a renaissance of vertical integration can be observed in many industries, with customers buying suppliers. The primary objective is to secure availability of short capacities and access to scarce resources. In special cases, the motivation may also be an anticipated technological competitive advantage or the ability to gain access to new customer groups. Besides these primary effects, vertical integration may also provide benefits in connection with transactions, logistics, dealerships etc.

Besides ensuring that the acquisition is commercially justified, one must always keep in mind that acquiring a supplier also means taking over its customers. It is therefore possible that, in a roundabout way, the buyer will also become the supplier of its own competitors. If this new state of affairs causes competitors to stop buying, the newly acquired supplier may be deprived of its business base.

Case example: Change of steel supplier through takeover of a service center

A medium-sized automotive supplier had sales of approx. 300 million US dollars, with steel purchases amounting to some 50 million US dollars. The steel was mostly sourced through regional service centers, as the company was too small to communicate directly with steel producers. The accelerating rise in steel prices was an increasing cause of concern as it directly impacted the business result. The solution was to take over a service center with sales of 300 million US dollars. By pooling steel for several dozen other companies through the service center, the company now commands enough volume to be able to talk to steel producers directly. This produces substantial advantages, i.e. better terms and better availability.

A7 Core cost analysis

What is a cheap car? If this question had been put to a European engineer ten years ago, the answer would probably have been: one costing less than 20,000 US dollars. If the same question had been asked five years ago, the answer would have been a Dacia Logan for 5,000 US dollars. Today, the answer would presumably be: A Tata Nano, at a price of around 1,500 US dollars.

The different answers result from the varying methods used. The usual method is to look at the lowest-cost competitor. Tata adopted a different tack and asked: What are the minimum requirements that a car must fulfill (i.e. transporting four persons from A to B with protection from the weather) and nothing more?

The core cost analysis strategy proceeds similarly. Instead of trying to cut the costs of an existing product through incremental measures, the idea is to start with a blank sheet of paper and ask what basic requirements the product must fulfill and what the cost structures would look like under ideal manufacturing conditions. The result is usually costs up to 40 to 60 percent below the actual figures. The next step is to move towards reality again by asking:

- Which additional features are customers prepared to pay for?
- What measures are necessary for risk management?
- What production processes are actually available?
- What suppliers are available?

Even after these concessions, the cost is usually still 20 to 30 percent below that of current products. This strategy seriously questions existing structures and calls for completely new ways of thinking. Thus purchasing, which has particularly close contact with alternative solutions through its contacts to suppliers, is ideally suited for driving this process.

Case example: Core cost analysis to reduce the purchase price of a control unit

A leading worldwide manufacturer of industrial control units was receiving ever-louder complaints from sales and marketing about the poor competitiveness of its basic product line. Since product management and development failed to provide any convincing impulses, purchasing was entrusted with cutting costs. It soon became clear to purchasing that, with the given specifications, there was nothing to be done using traditional methods. It therefore decided to perform a comprehensive, core cost analysis.

A series of workshops were held with sales and product management to determine the absolute minimum requirements customers would be prepared to accept. The list of insights that resulted from this was impressive:

- On/off switch eliminated.
- Only one of two connection alternatives (instead of both).
- DC connection eliminated.
- Service interface eliminated.

- Superfluous bus port eliminated.
- Thinner leads.
- Simpler plugs.
- Additional corrosion proofing eliminated.
- One board instead of two.
- Cold-start capability transferred to the system level.

The resulting core costs amounted to only 35 percent of the original costs. Management and sales were delighted. In a joint effort, most of these strategies were adopted in serial production. As a result, the basic product line has regained its expected cash-cow status.

A8 Invention on demand

Patent-protected suppliers are a particular challenge for purchasing. The traditional sourcing strategies are ineffective with these suppliers, who are able to demand just about any price for their product. Simply ignoring the patent protection and in-sourcing the product or having it produced by another supplier would be one option. However, the countless and sometimes very expensive patent lawsuits stand as a clear warning against this approach. Nevertheless, purchasing directors are increasingly looking around for alternatives to patent-protected suppliers. One such strategy is "invention on demand." This is based on TRIZ, an expression that comes from Russian and stands for "theory of inventive problem-solving." TRIZ utilizes basic empirical laws of inventive thinking and provides a wealth of systematic problem-solving tools.

The invention on demand model of solving problems comprises four steps:

1. Evaluation of the specific technical problem: The technical system is broken down into its smallest elements, and the functional relationships between these elements are depicted in graphic form. This functions model focuses on the end-result or end-product of the technical system. All other elements are assigned a functional ranking, which takes account of the distance to the end-product and a balancing of their useful and detrimental functions. The closer an element is to the product and the more useful functions it possesses, the higher its functional ranking.

2. Translation of the specific technical problem into a general scientific problem: Starting with the one with the lowest functional ranking (i.e. the least useful element), the elements are systematically eliminated. This makes contradictions in the technical system visible, i.e. it generates general scientific questions such as: "How can the useful functions of the eliminated element be performed in the absence of that element?" or "How can the remaining elements be made to assume the useful functions of the eliminated element?"

3. Search for general scientific solutions: The contradictions are systematically resolved. To do this, algorithms are used to search widely diverse areas of physics for potential solutions. This produces a number of ideas – some of them highly exotic – for each of the eliminated elements. These ideas are typically very general in nature and allow for wide scope in implementation. Bundling of these ideas leads to hundreds of rough concepts. At this stage, it is crucial that none of the rough concepts be prematurely discarded.

On the contrary, completeness is one of the key aspects of an invention on demand project, and ensures the ability of pursuing all possible solutions.

4. Translation of general scientific solutions into specific technical solutions. The last step in a project of this kind is to develop the rough concepts further into specific and viable technical solutions. To do this, the rough concepts are subjected to review in intense discussions with those in responsibility for the various corporate functions involved. This allows the insights of developers, product managers, marketing, and naturally also purchasing, to be taken into account. At this stage, resistance is not uncommon. To reach the optimum solution, strong leadership is therefore necessary. As the outcome of careful analysis, one or two dozen rough concepts will usually emerge. These are then transformed into commercially developable concepts, most of which are capable of being patented. The duration of a typical invention on demand project, from kick-off to commercially developable product, is three to four months.

The results of a project of this kind may be utilized in many different ways. Some companies use them to build critical capabilities internally. Most use the alternative concepts as a lever for negotiating with their current supplier. Through invention on demand, a company can in some cases not only solve the problem of patent-protected suppliers, but also replace expensive components with cheaper ones.

Case example: Circumvention of a patent by a French automotive supplier

Within the scope of a purchasing project, the team and the purchasing director discussed whether component A should be included in the product range. The purchasing director advised caution: "It would be better to leave it well enough alone. To my knowledge, the supplier has applied for patents for component A in Europe, Japan, and North America. So far, that didn't really matter to us because we only needed component A for one small-volume product. However, the sales figures for this product have risen sharply, and the latest market forecasts indicate even stronger growth in the coming year. That would mean we would become increasingly dependent on that one supplier. So we need to take urgent action to prevent that."

The team contacted a patent lawyer, who indicated a number of options. "Basically, there are the following possibilities: We could challenge the patent on the grounds that it infringes an existing patent. However, it is highly doubtful whether such a patent could be found. Moreover, the lawsuit could drag on for years. During that time, the supplier could create all kinds of difficulties. Alternatively, we could circumvent the patent. We would then have to get around at least one of the patent's claims. In other words, we would have to significantly alter one of component A's key characteristics. However, that change would have to be technically motivated, i.e. the modification must improve the functionality of the product. A purely "cosmetic" modification to the component would never hold in a patent court."

Following this briefing, the sourcing category team held a brainstorming session to consider the various solution strategies:

- "We need someone to carry out a functional analysis on component A, identify its drawbacks and develop a new and better technical approach."

- "You mean another supplier in the automotive industry?"

- "No, I don't think we could find an alternative solution within our industry. Everybody in our line of business works with component A. What we need is something completely new, a new way of looking at things, a new approach. The best thing would be to use top people from the scientific world."

- "Perhaps we could persuade Russian scientists to come on board. I've heard that people who formerly worked in aerospace and armaments are offering their services for product innovations in the private sector."

Following up on this idea, a bit of internet research quickly opened up a completely new perspective. It was possible to find a whole network of Russian scientists and engineers. This Russian team was highly impressive, not only on account of the references they could provide from a wide range of industries, but also due to their highly methodical approach to problem solving. Their goal was not so much to come up with new inventions, as to transfer tried and tested discoveries from one industry to another. Inventing was too uncertain a business, the scientists explained.

So the Russian team began to work with component A. After only a short time, the functional analysis was complete. To everyone's amazement, the scientists were able to find no less than 53 drawbacks in component A. But that was not all. Another eight weeks later, one of the Russian scientists presented 20 alternatives to the current design. All 20 alternatives fulfilled the following criteria:

- They were all financially and technically feasible.
- They did not infringe the patent for component A.
- They embodied some considerable improvements over component A.
- They were all separately patentable.

These alternatives could be used in renegotiations with the existing supplier. Although this created short-term savings, it did not fundamentally solve the problem of a patent-protected supplier. Therefore, some of the 20 alternatives were developed internally until they were ready for serial production. The potential benefits derivable from the introduction of a successful alternative were very difficult to assess in advance.

B1 Contract management

Even the best contracts are of little use if nobody is familiar with them. It often happens, especially in the larger conglomerates, that one group company concludes a contract without anyone in the rest of the group knowing anything about it. Contract management has the aim of creating transparency with regard to existing contracts throughout the company, as well as consolidating contracts, thus achieving better terms for all internal customers.

However, a number of basic rules must be observed:

- A contract must apply to all: The contract should include a clause making the terms of the contract available to all the group companies.

- Contracts must be easily accessible: An optimum method for achieving this is the use of intranet solutions, so that the contracts can be accessed from all sites of the corporate group.

- The product users/internal users of third-party services must be informed of the implemented intranet solution. Contract management of this kind is often implemented centrally; the head office is pleased with the progress, but the whole system fails to work because it has not been brought to the attention of users. To remedy this, a broad-based information policy is necessary.

- The product users/internal users of third-party services must be able to work easily with the intranet solution: This ranges from obtaining access authorizations without a lot of red tape all the way to being offered adequate training.

- The implemented system must be user-friendly. It is not sufficient to simply file master agreements centrally. The system must also offer search functions and include an automatic notification of updates.

- Feedback must be possible: When purchasing staff start using the system and the master agreements on a large scale, they must have the option of giving feedback and suggesting improvements without encountering red tape. Otherwise the system will never really be accepted by product users/internal users of third-party services.

> *Case example: Company cars for an energy provider*
>
> A major energy provider concluded a master agreement for the sourcing of company vehicles, but this fact was not properly communicated and was therefore unknown at the decentralized subsidiaries. The vehicles for the subsidiaries were therefore bought locally – until the master agreement was made generally available and communicated to internal users through a broad-based information campaign. The terms were three percent better on average than those agreed locally, but the agreement still allowed the vehicles to be procured through local dealerships. Thus purchasing quickly changed track and achieved the intended savings.

B2 Closed loop spend management

Many companies have substantially intensified their sourcing efforts during the last few years, with sometimes remarkable outcomes. Nevertheless, the sustained effect on results has often fallen short of expectations. Closed loop spend management offers a holistic approach developed in order to address "value destroyers" in a manner geared to the specific sourcing situation.

The challenge usually lies in the fact that purchasing has real influence on only a very small segment of the value-creation process. In the case of direct materials, for instance, purchasing usually becomes involved only after specifications have already been defined by the technical division. The purchaser has some leeway in the selection of supplier and in the conclusion of the contract, but has little influence on the subsequent process. Moreover, there is often a lack of transparency with regard to how demand planning is done, when the order is actually placed, when the goods are received, and when the invoices are paid.

The aim of closed loop spend management is to optimize expenses throughout the value-creation process and to generate sustainable value for the company. In a targeted analysis for specific product groups, potential value destroyers (imperfect spend transparency, demand management, user and supplier compliance, payment management, and process costs) are identified and concrete measures initiated.

Successful companies have established closed loop spend management as an end-to-end process within the responsibility of purchasing. Thus, purchasing is given not just the required information but also the power to implement necessary measures together with product users, internal users of third-party services, and those with functional responsibility.

> *Case example: Payables management at an industrial conglomerate*
>
> As part of a major purchasing project, closed loop spend management was applied in order to assure the sustainability of the savings achieved. This included a closer analysis of payables owed to suppliers. Special attention was paid to when the suppliers issued their invoices, what payment terms the invoices were based on, whether the payment terms corresponded to those agreed in the contract, and when payment was actually made. As a result, numerous cases were found in which payment terms deviated from those contractually agreed. For example, remittance was sometimes made more than 15 days before the final due date, without any cash discount being taken.

B3 Mega supplier strategy

It sometimes happens that two divisionally structured groups of companies have a mutual business volume worth dozens of millions of US dollars, but are virtually unaware of this fact. This can happen when the customer-supplier relationship is handled on a decentralized basis on both sides – e.g. when a local profit center of the supplier serves a local profit center of the customer. If these profit centers do not operate under the group name and the sourcing volume is spread over many different product groups, it can be challenging, even with the best intentions, to determine just how big the business volume actually is.

If most of these relationships are not on the radar screen of top-management at both groups, it will be extremely difficult to achieve any real optimization at the level of purchasing. This is precisely where the mega supplier strategy comes in. By making the huge purchasing volume transacted with a big, divisionally structured supplier ("mega supplier") transparent, the n:m relationship is turned into a 1:1 relationship.

The essential step in creating a mega supplier strategy is to determine the mutual interests of both sides. This means determining the degree of dependence on the mega supplier for each product group and identifying the special concerns associated with each group. These concerns may encompass a large number of topics, from the urgent need to cut costs to a requirement for product innovations. In return, scenarios for future business development will have to be presented to the mega supplier. These scenarios can range from the total loss of a prestigious reference customer to highly attractive sales growth.

Following an internal consultation process, the customer's top-management must then meet with that of the mega supplier. If the meeting is well prepared, it usually turns out to the customer's advantage.

> *Case example: Mega supplier strategy for a global paper manufacturer*
>
> A global paper manufacturer operates paper factories in nearly all parts of the world. The group's head office repeatedly attempted to bundle demand for a large number of product groups in the electrical equipment and automation technology field, but failed due to a lack of interest on the part of the factories. In the face of rising raw material prices, the factories were not prepared to concern themselves with "trivia" like the prices for spare parts or small investment programs.
>
> The head office persisted and, as a matter of urgency, put a group-wide purchasing information system in place. After many iteration loops, an astonishing outcome emerged. Across all sites and across 17 product groups, a leading electronics and automation technology company turned out to be one of the group's biggest suppliers. Purchasing volumes for the last three years, which fluctuated sharply from year to year, amounted to no less than 500 million US dollars.
>
> Armed with this information and a lengthy wish list, the paper manufacturer's CEO met the supplier's CEO. They already knew each other from the World Economic Forum in Davos, where they had had an intense discussion on the significance of state funds and then discovered over cocktails that they shared a love of twelve-tone music. But at that time, neither had realized that they were among each other's top 10 suppliers or top 30 customers!

B4 Buying consortia

Buying consortia are cooperations between companies that operate jointly on the sourcing market. Buying consortia normally take the form of horizontal pooling arrangements – i.e. purchasing volumes are bundled with those of competitors who are working jointly on a major project. Special trust between the companies involved is not necessary; it is sufficient for all parties to consistently support the project goals.

Organizationally speaking, various types of buying consortia are conceivable. One promising approach involves coordinated, internal or external networks of purchasing managers who consult and coordinate with each other periodically throughout the project. This enables sub-projects to be distributed among several experts.

As well as achieving better terms, buying consortia may also aim at pooling the know-how of partners so as to best fulfill the specific requirements of the project. The primary goal will normally be to safeguard the security of supply.

Case example: Purchasing consortium during construction of the Elbtunnel (a tunnel under the Elbe river)

The Elbtunnel at Hamburg (Germany) is one of Europe's most important north-south highway connections, carrying virtually the whole of the traffic from Denmark and northern Germany to the South. Since the first two tubes were built in the 1970s, the volume of traffic has almost doubled. In the 1970s, when the tunnel went into operation, it was designed for

> 70,000 vehicles per day; by the 1990s, the traffic volume had reached nearly 120,000 vehicles per day. To relieve the pressure on this traffic axis, the construction of a fourth tunnel tube was commissioned by the German Federal Ministry of Transport, Building and Urban Affairs as owner and the City of Hamburg as contract manager. The fourth Elbtunnel tube was designed as a tunnel crossing below the river Elbe. The contract volume amounted to some 445 million euros.
>
> For the coordination and implementation of this investment, a joint venture by the name of "ARGE 4. Röhre Elbtunnel Hamburg" was founded, comprising the companies Hochtief, Bilfinger+Berger, Dyckerhoff & Widmann AG, Heitkamp, Philip Holzmann AG, Wayss & Freitag, and Ed. Züblin AG. The partners each performed precisely defined complementary services (e.g. overall project management by Hochtief and construction of the protective shell for the tunnels by Bilfinger + Berger). In a constricted construction site like a tunnel tube, just the material logistics by themselves required the coordinated involvement of the suppliers.

B5   Political framework management

The deregulation of the telecommunications and air travel markets in Europe has led to undreamt-of competition and low prices. Without the corresponding regulatory interventions, purchasers on these supplier's markets would still be in a very difficult negotiating position today.

In exactly the same way, regional oligopolies can be broken open through the lifting of import duties (e.g. on steel from Asia). If illegal cartels or price agreements are suspected, an individual company also has the possibility to contact and involve the antitrust authorities. Similarly, close cooperation with the competition authorities in advance of a planned merger has the aim of preempting too much concentration on the supplier side (and hence excessive supply power). Suppliers will also often attempt to establish their own technologies as standard and thus restrict the customer's freedom. The customer must take timely action in order to nip these kinds of efforts in the bud.

Left to its own devices, a company generally has little power to influence the political framework conditions. It is therefore important for a company to know exactly what it wants to achieve and then work consistently towards this goal by lobbying in industrial associations, mobilizing others who share the same views, and carrying out targeted media work. If done correctly, political framework management has the ability to shift the balance between supply and demand power like no other strategy.

> *Case example: Cheaper telephone calls through liberalization of the telecom market*
>
> For decades, telecommunications were the domain of state monopolies. Prices were based directly on costs and were ordained by the state – customers had no possibility to negotiate. Today, the telecom sector is one of the most competitive of all. New terrestrial network operators are constantly appearing, while mobile telephone providers are in a price war with one another. In the last 10 years, the prices of telecommunications have fallen by an average of 80 percent, with purchasers able to choose from a large number of operators with highly differentiated offers. Through changes in the political framework conditions, the balance of power has undergone a fundamental shift, from being a seller's market to a buyer's market.

B6 Intelligent deal structure

Especially on a seller's market, the careful drafting of contracts is of paramount importance. Well-produced contracts can be a significant competitive advantage in that they ensure the availability of capacities and resources in the face of scarce supplies, thus helping to ensure growth. Similarly, in situations of surging raw material prices, contracts can help to ensure that budgets are met.

In drafting the appropriate contract structure, the first step is to identify the risk position. This involves determining how high the exposure of the company is (i.e. what proportion of sales revenues, costs, or net income would be affected), and how controllable the influencing factors are. This risk position then forms the basis for defining a goal.

If the goal is "planning certainty over the budget period", this can be achieved through hedging. Depending on the company's appetite for risk, various instruments exist. The three most important are as follows:

- Swap – a fixed price is agreed independently of the actual market price.

- Cap – only an upper limit is placed on market price fluctuations; if prices fall, the company can take full advantage of them.

- Collar – a range is defined, within which prices can follow the market fluctuations.

One thing all these hedging instruments have in common is that they merely delay, but do not prevent, the effects of permanent rises in raw material prices, and that they naturally give rise to costs. Nevertheless, airlines that undertook aviation fuel hedging are in a much healthier economic position than competitors who did not. To cope with rises in raw material prices over the long term, however, it is necessary to pass these higher costs on to suppliers or customers – once again, with the aid of intelligent contracts.

If "supply security" is the goal derived from the risk position, then implementation calls for even more creativity than in the case of hedging. Drafting contracts that can secure capacities on a tight market is anything but easy, since they have to combine security with flexibility. They must also include reliable rolling forecasts of demand in order to provide suppliers with transparency about the volumes that will be required in future. When preparing such contracts, the following must be asked:

- What price mode applies in the case of reservations?
- What is the time span for confirming/canceling/postponing a reservation?
- On what terms can a reservation be canceled/postponed?
- What pledges apply in the case of "rolling" forecasts?

Case example: Material inflation surcharges in the automobile industry

Herbert Diess, BMW Purchasing and Supplier Networks Director, complained in an interview with "Automobilwoche" magazine that BMW's suppliers had succeeded in passing on increased raw material costs to BMW at a rate of 100 percent – or in some cases even as much as 110 percent – and that this had severely depressed BMW's results.

> As a consequence, it has now been announced that material inflation surcharges will be split. In future, a so-called "1/3 clause" is to be introduced into contracts with suppliers. To make sure that all members of the value-creation chain share in the rise in material costs, the "1/3 clause" specifies that one third of material price rises must be borne by BMW, one third by BMW's direct suppliers, and one third by pre-suppliers.

B7 Design for sourcing

The majority of supplier monopolies are brought about by customers themselves. According to investigations by A.T. Kearney, two out of every three situations in which only one supplier was able to fulfill a customer's requirements arose not because of the supplier's proprietary technologies, but due to the customer's own actions.

The main causes of such self-caused supplier monopolies are departmental goals that deviate from the company's corporate strategy. The R&D department, for example, will often exclusively pursue the goal of creating a product as near to perfection as possible. Production, on the other hand, will be primarily interested in a lean-assembly process, while the aim of purchasing will be to buy from as few suppliers as possible at the lowest prices. In themselves, all these departmental goals are perfectly valid, but taken together they can drive a company to ruin.

A clever supplier takes advantage of this mix of departmental goals by tailoring a special solution for the company in question, thus drawing as much development and production know-how as possible into his own hands. After a few years, the customer is completely dependent on the supplier.

In order to remedy this situation, an interdisciplinary effort is required. First, one must determine whether the item supplied by the supplier is a differentiating factor for the end product or not. If not, it can be replaced by a standard industrial article. If the product is a differentiating factor, however, the solution is often more complicated. In this case, it is necessary to create the required development competence internally so as to regain control of the process. One must then develop a solution that meets the expectations of end customers at least as well as the current solution. At the same time, the new solution must offer greater freedom to maneuver on the supplier market.

Case example: A crane manufacturer

During a slump in sales ten years ago, a crane manufacturer was forced to outsource a considerable part of its production to suppliers in order to reduce its cost base. In the process, one of the core items of its crane technology – the locking mechanism located on the telescopic cylinder – also found its way to the outside. (The locking mechanism is what enables a large telescopic crane to move all segments of the telescope arm with just one cylinder.) The supplier of the telescopic cylinder was very much interested in taking over the production of the locking mechanism, and was awarded a corresponding contract.

The benefits anticipated from outsourcing production of the locking mechanism were fully achieved. Production profited most, as the labor-intensive job of assembling the locking mechanism was no longer needed, and the supplier even delivered the locking mechanism pre-assembled as one unit, together with the telescopic cylinder. It was also possible to cut back the development staff.

> The supplier used the following years to improve and enhance the complete telescopic cylinder and locking system, and even applied for (and was granted) certain patents. As a result, the crane manufacturer was now completely dependent on the supplier. After years of booming business, the crane manufacturer eventually wanted to regain its freedom of action and take advantage of highly attractive offers from other cylinder makers. However, it had to work hard to recover and update its know-how with regard to the locking mechanism, which it had almost completely lost. The company was fortunate in that one of the employees who had played a key role in developing the locking mechanism was still on its payroll.

B8 Leverage innovation network

How many people in a company are engaged in finding innovations? An average SME company with sales of around $1 billion has around 50 core employees working on R&D. Such a company also works with 200 core suppliers. If the company can get just one developer at each of these suppliers to think about innovations, the number of "brains" at work is increased fivefold at just one stroke!

This is the underlying idea behind innovation networks. At a time when competitive pressure is high and engineers in short supply, innovation networks are increasingly important. The benefits are obvious: Companies with successful innovation management enjoy stronger and more profitable growth. The best starting point for an innovation network are the suppliers, since they are well acquainted with the needs of the company and the industry as a whole. Besides suppliers, innovation networks often include customers, competitors, research institutes, market researchers, business consultants and former employees.

Within the company, the innovation process involves not just R&D and purchasing, but many other units as well, i.e. marketing/PR, sales and distribution, production, quality, trend scouts, service, plus the company's top-management.

Thus, an innovation network enables development to acquire insights into new technologies. These insights can then help the company free itself from dependence on suppliers. For an innovation network to be effective, the following features are essential:

- Innovations must be driven top-down as an integral part of corporate strategy.

- The innovation strategy and search fields must be clearly defined (in writing).

- Receptiveness towards innovative ideas must be a pillar of the corporate culture.

- Close collaboration must be fostered, as well as internal/external networking.

- The ideas pipeline must be actively managed.

- With regard to process and product technologies, a high level of company-wide standardization and reutilization must be the norm.

- Goals must be systematically pursued and structures established for learning from experience.

- HR tools must be used to help integrate innovations.

In companies that are innovation leaders, structured processes are used for evaluating ideas. A number of factors have proved successful in this context. First, it is important to make systematic use of all ideas and their sources. Great weight and care must be accorded to pre-qualifying ideas so as to avoid tying up resources unnecessarily. Also, feedback should be given on every idea within a short time (approx. six weeks). To enable an actual decision to be reached quickly within the evaluation process, a special governance structure should be introduced, whereby web-based technologies can also be helpful.

Case example: Time-triggered (TT) Ethernet for Orion

There is no doubt that Honeywell is a highly qualified partner for the aerospace industry. Honeywell components may not always be visible, but the company is right at the heart of US and international aerospace programs. For decades now, Honeywell has supplied mission-critical systems for the Space Shuttle and the International Space Station (ISS), and most recently for the new Boeing 777 and Airbus A380.

Despite – or because of – this impressive array of experience, Honeywell maintains a professionally managed innovation network, which brought Honeywell in contact with a young Austrian company, TTTech. The outcome was remarkable: Thanks to its cooperation with TTTech, Honeywell was able to dramatically improve the connection and processing of critical real-time data.

This in turn enabled Honeywell to win a contract to equip the Space Shuttle's successor, "Orion". Thus, Honeywell will continue to be right at the heart of the US space program in coming decades as well.

Bundling across product lines

"Have we gone completely crazy?" According to *"Manager Magazin"* (a leading German business magazine) this was the reaction of BMW's CEO Norbert Reithofer in May 2008 when confronted with the company's dozens of different wing mirrors and V-belt pulleys, as well as its 27 different cooling units.

However, BMW is not alone in this regard, for developers apparently find it easier to design a new component from scratch rather than to look around for existing ones to incorporate into a new product. The deep-seated human ambition to create something new and individual evidently plays a major role in this context.

And yet the rational approach of using the same components across various product lines makes sense. The benefits offered by scale effects, with resulting lower prices for parts, simplified logistics and more efficient repairs, are obvious. The only question is how to actually implement bundling across product lines.

The simplest case is when the same components are already in use across several product lines, but are being bought at different prices. Here, potential savings can be easily realized. As a rule, however, components only resemble one another in function, but differ in terms of performance, size, connections and so on. Thus, it is only possible to achieve isolated, minor successes for the current product generation, and even this will require concentrated, interdisciplinary effort.

True bundling across product lines calls for a long-term visionary concept in which the strategies for modules, platforms and part-sharing are clearly defined. Once this concept is in place, all product development projects must be undertaken in accordance with the new guidelines.

Case example: The platform strategy of a major automotive OEM

A prominent example of successful bundling across product lines is the Volkswagen platform strategy. The early 1990s marked the start of Ferdinand Piëch's tenure at the helm of the Volkswagen Group. At that time, VW was beset by both profitability and quality problems. Piëch identified the root cause as an excessively high level of technical complexity. His response: the "platform strategy". Instead of developing each new model from scratch, the components of a car were broken down into two fundamentally different categories: Those the customer sees ("hat parts") and those the customer does not see ("platform parts"). Platform parts account for about 60 percent of the costs and R&D input in a car. The idea of the strategy was to develop platform parts to perfection only once, and then fit a wide variety of different "hats" on top. As a consequence, the VW models Golf, Vento and New Beetle, the Skoda Octavia, the Audi models A3 and TT, and the Seat models Leon and Toledo all ran on the same platform.

The benefits of the platform were limited not just to cost reductions. Thanks to the high volumes involved, it was possible to use components of fundamentally higher quality, and thus enhance product quality as a whole. This approach also enabled product development times to be cut dramatically, with new models coming to market in about half the time needed before. Since then, Volkswagen has taken the platform strategy even further. The basic idea has stayed the same, however. It has not only revolutionized the automobile industry as a whole, but has also been adopted by many other industries – even software companies now refer to their "platform strategies."

C2 Supplier consolidation

A paradox frequently observed is that companies often depend on a monopolistic supplier for items crucial for success, while they maintain relations with a large number of suppliers for standard items. Here, action must be taken to reverse the situation. Too many suppliers for uncritical items tie up resources; they distract from issues of real importance and are ultimately not even able to produce good prices. Thus, supplier consolidation means, above all, eliminating smaller suppliers by shifting to bigger or strategically important ones. This creates savings through economies of scale. But savings also result from the need to maintain less supplier data and fewer contacts in the system. The procedure for supplier consolidation comes from the basic purchasing toolbox:

- Collecting data (who buys what from which supplier) for at least 80 percent of sourcing volume.

- Leveraging competition from existing and new suppliers.

- Negotiating with interested, qualified and competitive suppliers.

- Choosing the preferred future suppliers on the basis of cogent criteria.

- Changing over to these preferred suppliers in a consistent manner.

The success of this measure depends first and foremost on being open towards new suppliers and willing to give up cherished habits (e.g. favoring suppliers who maintain a high profile and take care of the little things, but charge a high price for it).

> *Case example: Pallet purchasing by a producer of consumer goods*
>
> A producer of consumer goods with eight plants in Germany, Belgium and Denmark used a total of 49 suppliers for its wooden pallets; many of these were local suppliers who were able to respond quickly to short-term needs.
>
> As part of a purchasing project, the main pallet types were put up for bidding. Czech and Polish suppliers emerged as winners from the subsequent negotiating phase, which was significantly shortened by a reverse auction. Testing, conducted in the face of resistance from within the company, confirmed the high product quality and supply security of the new suppliers. With the strong support of the managing board, the pallets were placed almost completely in the hands of two suppliers. The only exception was one of the old suppliers, who could be counted upon to fill unscheduled demand at short notice. Thus, only three suppliers are now being used, instead of the previous 49.

C3 Master data management

Nobody knowingly builds his house on sand. Nevertheless, the master data of many companies is in a pitiable state. This means that all the systems, evaluations, sourcing strategies and reported savings based on such unreliable master data are very much like houses built on sand.

Purchasing, for its part, draws on data from a large number of subsystems in order to compile comprehensive information on suppliers, demand and supply factors, payment terms and prices. Hitch-free master data management is thus a major prerequisite for bringing transparency into purchasing data. Master data management encompasses the standardized classification of material and supplier data, consistent linking between master data and the ordering system, and the avoidance of free-text ordering.

Many companies face considerable challenges in this process. This is because the role of data management is often restricted to that of mere administration, while the master data structure is often non-standardized insofar as the company was created through merger or acquisition.

These challenges can be tackled by master data management, which is especially important for groups of materials not shown in parts lists, including indirect materials such as lubricants, occupational health and safety items, or spare parts.

The first priority in optimizing a company's master data management is to review the quality of data. This involves ascertaining the extent of coverage the maintained master data provides, the data's level of detail, the volume of inactive data present in the system, and the extent to which harmonization of individual data systems is ensured. This is followed by an analysis of the categorization systems, the required level of detail and the appropriate solution for categorization. The sorting and restructuring process, undertaken with the aid of innovative and intelligent tools, encompasses the following:

Classification system

- Limitation of the categorization possibilities.
- Introduction of sustainable and understandable logic.
- Avoidance of gaps for particular sectors.

- Avoidance of the category "Miscellaneous".
- Clear demarcation between categories.

Material master data

- Classification of all materials and services.
- Link-up between electronic catalogs and the classification system.
- Link-up between suppliers and material groups.

Orders

- Avoiding orders with free-text entry.
- Obligating users to use valid keywords for categorization.
- Manual review of orders.

This is followed by an analysis and definition of the process for specifying, deleting, amending and administering master data, as well as of functions and responsibilities. The results can be used as a basis for spend transparency, purchasing management and sustainability of savings.

> *Case example: Improving master data at a producer of fast-moving consumer goods*
>
> The company, which grew largely through acquisitions, operated for a long time purely as a holding company, restricting itself to consolidation of financial results. After the group had grown to over 40 firms, top-management determined that the next growth phase required transformation into an integrated industrial enterprise. It was therefore planned that the various firms would be gradually merged with regards to development, purchasing, production and logistics.
>
> Management was well aware that the first requirement for this step was a sound database. In a project implemented without external support, a categorization system was created and made available via the intranet. Instructions were then issued to the top-managers of the 40 firms to make categorization of master data their top priority. The group's COO instructed top-managers to provide him with weekly progress reports. After only four months, the group had master data of a quality that could stand comparison with that of any company in the world. On this solid foundation, the group then embarked on a purchasing project that produced millions of dollars worth of savings.

C4 Cost data mining

In many cases, customers will raise the issue of payment terms, bonus agreements and discount rates right at the end of negotiations with suppliers, in the hope of obtaining some small additional concession. Once obtained, however, these benefits are often never exploited, either because differing agreements are in place within the group or because of a lack of transparency.

In this situation, a thorough analysis of cost data can help. In the "cost data mining" approach, data available internally on purchased products and services is exploited for potential savings. In the process, one often discovers much more savings potential than originally expected. The specific procedure is to analyze the cost data from various angles in order to identify correlations or patterns among the dozens of fields in the internal databases. To this end, the fields are organized in clusters and associations are formed. Some examples:

- Comparing bonus agreements between suppliers and categories.
- Comparing discount rates between suppliers and categories.
- Comparing payment terms between suppliers and categories.
- Comparing delivery terms and delivery times between suppliers and sites.
- Comparing rejection levels between product lines and suppliers.
- Comparing the wear or service life of products between suppliers.

Case example: Cost data mining for the purchasing of processing tools

For a manufacturer of steel structures, indexable inserts are one of the most important tools used in the milling and drilling of steel parts. There are numerous types of indexable inserts, which are offered on the basis of

> an extensive catalog. Purchasing's primary task is to negotiate discounts for the product groups bought from the catalog.
>
> A comparison of the discount lists was precisely what provided the main impetus for savings. After collecting all the discount lists agreed within the group, a comparison was carried out and used to identify the best group-wide terms. As a result, it was possible to achieve savings of between five and ten percent in subsequent group-wide negotiations with suppliers.

C5 Product benchmark

Product benchmark is a method for cutting the costs of products of limited technical complexity, whereby the focus is on the specifications and the production process. A tried-and-tested product benchmark process can be broken down into four steps:

- Identification of comparable products: The initial step is the identification and procurement of comparable products from competitors. To identify competitors' products, it is necessary to interview sales, development, customers and suppliers. The competitors' catalogs are also evaluated. The outcome is a list of relevant competing products.

- Evaluation of competing products: The individual products are compared, with the assistance of development and production. Each product is rated according to functionality, technology, usability, and compliance with specifications and dimensions. Products unable to meet internal requirements are eliminated at this stage.

- Inviting bids for existing products and alternatives: Suppliers are invited to tender offers for existing products and appropriate alternatives. As part of the tender process, suppliers are advised of possible design solutions that could be adopted from competitors. Especially for alternative products, it is crucial that the process includes new suppliers along with existing ones.

- Analysis of results: The final step is to analyze the results and identify potential cost savings. Individual alternatives must be prioritized on the basis of feasibility and potential. For high-priority offers, the next steps of implementation must also be identified.

Product benchmark allows various alternatives available on the market to be compared quickly and with relatively little effort. The involvement of purchasing, development, sales and suppliers is crucial, but should be strictly limited time-wise. The results can normally be implemented rapidly, insofar as it has already been determined that comparable products are available from suppliers. Product benchmark should be carried out right at the start of developing a new product, so that any necessary design changes can still be incorporated in time.

Case example: Product benchmark in sourcing counterweights for a crane

For cranes, counterweights are a key safety component. As a rule, the specifications for a counterweight only address dimensions and weight. The material is usually not specified, since counterweights are traditionally made of cast iron.

> With the aid of product benchmark, an attractive alternative was identified, consisting of a welded steel box filled with scrap and concrete. Further analysis showed that, in times of surging raw material prices, the steel/scrap/concrete combination was an effective cost-saving solution that still met all the specifications.

C6 Composite benchmark

Every company is interested in knowing what lies beneath the skin of competing products, so that it can make its own products even better and win over customers. However, many companies lack the resources and/or knowledge to perform the necessary analysis of a product and its components themselves. The idea of composite benchmark is to send a choice of competing products to several suppliers for expert examination. These analyses are often intensive, revealing information about a supplier's production costs. The result is a cost model of "the best product from the best supplier with the best production processes."

This approach is suitable for products consisting of a number of different (but not overly complex) components, insofar as a sufficient number of existing and potential suppliers can be recruited for the composite benchmark process.

A crucial factor for success is the make-up of the team, which should comprise specialists with both technical and commercial expertise. Composite benchmark is carried out in seven steps:

1. Agree on the approach with suppliers: First of all, one must identify new potential suppliers (besides the existing ones) on the basis of their product portfolios, competencies and capacities. To motivate suppliers to take part in the composite benchmark procedure, incentives should be offered. These may include exchange of technical information, opportunities for more business or the establishment of new business relationships. The incentives should be individualized for each supplier. It is also crucial to talk with the suppliers in advance about methodology, allocation of tasks, and expectations.

2. Identify appropriate competing products: An internal procedure should be used to identify competitors' products suitable for composite benchmark. Based on functional comparability, the best products are selected and purchased.

3. Produce standardized cost-calculation sheets: The various factors that go into cost calculations are materials, individual components and other processing steps.

4. Have the questionnaires edited by suppliers: Send the cost-calculation sheets to participating suppliers along with the competitors' products. Ask the suppliers to disassemble each product and evaluate the individual components along with the production steps needed to make them. At the end of this key phase, you will have questionnaires completed by the suppliers as well as offers for each product and its components.

5. Evaluate the offers: Incoming offers must be carefully compared with one other. It is essential to clarify any discrepancy with suppliers right away. Only then will the offers be genuinely comparable.

6. Identify potential savings: On the basis of the offers and the detailed cost calculation sheets provided by the suppliers, purchasing can now identify potential savings on three levels:

    ☐ Identification of the supplier with the lowest price for each of the products in the existing configuration.

    ☐ Reconfiguration of a product using components with the lowest costs.

    ☐ Identification of the lowest production costs. The optimum production costs for each combination of products are determined. To this end, the benchmark costs of the "best of the best" (with optimum functionalities and lowest manufacturing costs) are identified for the original product.

7. Implement the target costs: As a last step, the target costs are implemented with the aid of suppliers. Each supplier is provided with individual feedback as to where it stands in terms of target costs. In addition, improvements at both the component/production-process level are identified and discussed in detail.

The outcome of composite benchmark is a reliable analysis of comparable competing products. It allows for ambitious but realizable cost savings to be identified and directly implemented in negotiations with suppliers.

Case example: Benchmarking of wing mirrors for an automaker

An automaker decided to carry out composite benchmark for wing mirrors after managing to persuade four suppliers (two existing and two potential new ones) to participate. The team, consisting of personnel from engineering and purchasing, decided to include two products from direct competitors, along with two products from competitors in low-wage countries.

For the cost calculation sheets, the following components were identified: cover, hinge mechanism, adjusting knob, mount, frame, and mirror glass. The parts and materials were specified for each individual component. The suppliers were requested to state the costs for parts purchasing, personnel, materials, machine utilization at component level, as well as development costs included in overhead at product level. To ensure the procedure was properly understood, a joint workshop was held with the participating suppliers.

A few weeks later, results were available with regard to potential cost savings, optimum functionality and the cost-optimal production processes. Minor functional differences between competing products were also identified and evaluated financially. Negotiations and targeted feedback sessions were then held with each supplier. The savings potential identified in this way amounted to 27 percent in all, broken down as follows: 5 to 10 % for the cover, 15 to 25 % for the adjusting knob, 5 to 15 % for the frame, 25 to 30 % for the mirror glass, and 30 to 35% for additional indirect costs.

C7 Product teardown

Little boys take delight in pulling their new toy cars to pieces in order to find out how they work. R&D personnel do much the same thing when they analyze competing products in detail. In the case of product teardown, a product is disassembled completely into all of its constituent parts. Product teardown is a common method for analyzing the competition's products, and was developed in the 1960s by Japanese firms trying to understand how European cars and cameras worked. During product teardown, very careful attention is paid to the materials and components used and their costs. This form of analysis enables one to identify the best solutions employed by competitors.

The product teardown process consists of three steps:

1. Analysis of technical differences: First, the product is broken down into all of its individual components, which are precisely labeled. The suppliers of the individual components are identified. Then, differences between the company's own parts and the teardown components are recorded in detail, e.g. in terms of dimensions, weights and design approaches.

2. Analysis of possible technical improvement: Based on the results of step one, one then looks for optimization potential. All significant improvement possibilities are recorded in a list and reviewed for technical feasibility.

3. Identification of potential cost optimization: The possibilities identified in step two are discussed and assessed by an interdisciplinary team. This will often generate proposed modifications that require detailed technical validation. The outcome of this process is implementation of the modifications.

Case example: Product teardown by a washing machine manufacturer

Working on behalf of a leading manufacturer of household appliances, A.T. Kearney carried out a product teardown for washing machines. 15 out of 20 machines on the market were chosen and subjected to product teardown. Altogether, 60 different components were compared in detail. Each part was precisely weighed and measured, material tests were performed, manufacturer's designations noted and technical designs analyzed.

These comparisons provided the basis for a number of improvements. For instance, it was found that specially made components could be replaced by standard ones. Simply weighing the components was a source of highly interesting insights. The weight of the washing drum, for instance, could be reduced from 1.3 kg to 0.8 kg, after it was noted that all the competing drums weighed between 0.6 and 0.9 kg. The control units and wiring were also modified in the light of the best technical designs. All in all, material costs were reduced by 20 million US dollars – with the laundry coming out just as clean as before!

C8 Functionality assessment

How many of the functions offered by a mobile telephone does the typical user actually use? Or how many of the functions available in computer programs such as Microsoft Excel? Which of these functions provide genuine benefit for the typical user? What could the typical user do without, and what would he or she be prepared to pay for if they were not already included in the cell phone or computer program? In many cases, far too many functions are offered. Since this also creates excess costs, it makes sense to assess each function in detail.

Functionality assessment calls for an interdisciplinary team, consisting not just of purchasing staff but also of specialists from Engineering, Production and Sales. The process takes place in five steps:

1. Identification of functions: First, the product has to be broken down into its various sub-systems and components, and their respective functions identified.

2. Naming of the functions: Next, all the functions identified must be given a meaningful name. This should consist of two expressive words: an active verb and a measurable noun, which together clearly illustrate and define the significance of the individual components. Examples would be, "prevents corrosion", "positions parts" or "absorbs vibration."

3. Classification of functions: The functions are assigned to one of four classes: basic, critical, supporting and non-supporting functions.

4. Valuation of cost-function ratios: The valuation of cost-function ratios is essential for identifying potential improvements. The information is listed on an evaluation sheet along with all components and their functions. On each individual line, the relationship between part, function and cost is valued. Addition of all the columns produces total costs.

5. Identification of potential improvements: The following are general rules for identifying components to optimize: (a) the product can be viewed as cost-effective if the costs predominantly occur in the area

of basic or critical functions. (b) If significant costs are found in supporting functions, one can achieve savings without changing the basic concept. (c) The highest savings can be realized in non-supporting functions.

The above process enables potential to be identified, with a list of possible improvement measures as the outcome. However, the basic and critical functions should be reviewed as well in order to find alternative solutions, if appropriate.

> *Case example: Functionality assessment at an automaker*
>
> Many Europeans on vacation in the USA are surprised at the large number of young people who can afford a Ford Mustang. The surprise is even greater when they look at the price list: The car costs a mere 18,000 US dollars when new. The explanation is provided by the "functionality assessment" approach. During development, and even after completion of the Mustang prototype, specialists valued each of the car's functions, subjecting them to highly critical scrutiny. Among other things, the approach was applied to the engine cover (a plastic component that at first sight looks like the engine itself). What does the engine cover, what function does it have? It has minimal supporting functions and tends to be characterized mainly by non-supporting functions, such as aesthetics. Only a threaded hole on the cylinder head still bears witness to the fact that a component was originally fitted here. Nonetheless, the sales success of the Mustang on markets well beyond its original US target market proves the correctness of the "functionality assessment" approach.

D1 Bundling across sites

The principle of structuring companies by profit centers with local business responsibility is frequently applied by companies in both North America and Europe. As these companies are often highly successful, there is evidently nothing wrong with the principle as such.

Consulting practice shows, however, that the autonomy granted to the individual sites is often excessive, with the result that considerable savings potential remains unused. Also, the responsibility of profit centers for P & L is often taken to mean that they must handle all purchasing, given that purchased materials account for a high proportion of turnover (often over 50 percent). This way of thinking leads to a proliferation of sub-critical purchasing organizations, all working in parallel on the market. In many cases, the sites buy similar products, sometimes even from the same suppliers.

In order to identify potential savings, one must first talk to the individual site purchasers to find out precisely what demand which site has in terms of quantity and quality. Next, one must compile the necessary data to draw up a joint invitation to tender. The invitation is issued to all existing and new suppliers theoretically able to supply several sites. Negotiations are then conducted for all the participating sites at once. It is essential to decide in advance which sites should lead the negotiations and which ones should only participate in a supporting capacity. Conducting the negotiations need not be entrusted to the site with the highest demand, but rather to whichever one appears most capable. Thus, the chief negotiator should be a local purchaser who is especially well versed in the technology concerned and has expertise in the supplier market.

In many cases, a project for identifying savings potential across sites will form the core of a future lead-buyer structure. In this case, lead negotiators who previously acted in only an informal capacity will grow into an official organizational role and assume purchasing responsibility across sites. This responsibility may be restricted to simple market research, but may also include concluding master agreements or even taking overall charge of ordering.

Case example: Purchasing of paper by a packaging manufacturer

A leading worldwide manufacturer of flexible packaging products, such as yogurt tops and bottle labels, managed its over 50 worldwide sites on strict profit-center principles. The individual sites appeared to be operating in different fields with differing focal activities, e.g. in paper, plastic and aluminum. On closer inspection, however, it was found that virtually all sites bought significant volumes of paper, since paper is used together with plastic and aluminum in many different laminate structures.

The first step, therefore, was to harmonize the terminology used at different sites in order to understand how much paper and what type was being used across the entire company. This was followed by detailed analysis of the worldwide supplier market with the aim of identifying which suppliers could supply what range of products. As the market had already gone through a phase of consolidation, there were several suppliers offering a broad range. A joint invitation to tender was prepared; a joint negotiating strategy was drawn up and the best negotiating representatives were nominated by purchasing and engineering. By bundling demand and operating jointly on the market, it was possible to

> identify a number of attractive new suppliers, the most interesting being a highly innovative paper manufacturer with state-of-the-art facilities in China. The Chinese supplier passed the tests with flying colors and, even after allowing for logistics costs, still offered savings of well over ten percent. The Chinese supplier would never have been interested in the small volumes needed by the individual sites, and could only be won through the bundling of demand across the sites.

D2 Bundling across generations

Every company can bundle, even those with only one product and one site. How is that possible, one might ask? The answer: by bundling across product generations. This approach has practical applications above all in the project business. By definition, a project is an undertaking with a clear goal and an end. To avoid treating each project as an isolated, one-time affair and to succeed in bundling across generations, one must appeal to the entrepreneurial imagination of suppliers.

Even though only little negotiating strength may be associated with a current project, one can gain substantial concessions from a supplier through the prospect of inclusion in actual or possible future projects. If the supplier can supply the same products for future projects, it may even be possible for tooling and development costs to be amortized over several projects.

> *Case example: Engines for a tank-building program*
>
> Following an exhausting bidding phase, a producer of military tanks finally received the contract to equip a European army. During the bidding, an engine manufacturer with good contacts to the defense ministry had succeeded in getting its engine stipulated in the design specifications. The tank producer therefore had no choice but to buy the engines from this particular supplier. To make matters worse, the quantity required by the tank maker was very small compared to the number purchased by truck manufacturers, who basically used the same engine.
>
> A purchasing project was nevertheless set up to address this seemingly hopeless situation. First of all, the unit prices paid by truck manufacturers for comparable engines were researched. The difference was found to be 25 percent. The engine manufacturer was confronted with this fact but (understandably) saw no reason to go down with the price. Only when the tank producer presented a portfolio of future armament programs, indicating that these offered the possibility for further cooperation, was the engine maker prepared to reconsider. The price was eventually reduced by 18 percent.

D3 Spend transparency

Like parched travelers in the desert who chase after every mirage, many companies engage in massive SAP or Oracle projects, in the hopes of achieving a perfect integrated solution that can supply any desired corporate data at the press of a button. In this time of constant mergers and acquisitions, however, it is simply not possible to achieve the goal in this way. Large-scale IT projects will always lag behind corporate reality, and especially in the post-merger phase will never answer the question that most interests purchasing – who buys what from which supplier?

What is needed is an alternative solution that can provide precisely this information with the aid of a purchasing data cube using the three dimensions of "location," "product," and "supplier." The cube enables intersections to be made on all planes, and allows initial fundamental analyses to be carried out, e.g. identification of bundling potential between sites, comparisons of the number of suppliers, or the proportion of sourcing in countries with high cost factors. All the data needed for creating this sort of cube can already be found in the internal system. The cube itself can be created using various methods.

The choice of tools depends on the complexity of the company and the desired sustainability of the cube. If the company has a homogenous, uncomplicated structure, the data needed for the cube can normally be retrieved from existing systems using standard interfaces. In cases of this kind, the only tool normally needed is a standard spreadsheet program.

In heterogeneous and complex companies, on the other hand, highly sophisticated tools are often required. Many companies only produce a small volume on the basis of parts lists; these companies have much higher expectations with regard to data transparency. This is often accompanied by the wish to "dynamize" the cube, i.e. to update the data it contains at periodic intervals (often monthly). Thus, the cube acquires great importance as a management tool. As a periodically updated tool, it allows the tracking of purchasing at individual sites. In addition, purchasing management can use it to monitor compliance with master agreements. A purchasing data cube's capabilities can vary widely, with the expense involved differing accordingly.

Case example: Energy supplier

Based on SAP-BW technology, the purchasing data cube of a major energy supplier supports standardization at suppliers as well as consolidation of data through the use of innovative tools. Users can access the data via a web application. Data access is regulated by a strict authorization system.

The purchasing data cube has a highly impressive range of capabilities:

- Collection of local sourcing data in eleven languages from 26 physical ERP systems with data from 96 accounting groups.

- 30 gigabytes of data on twelve million invoices.

- Comparison/validation of data with P&L, balance sheets and accounts payable.

- 220,000 suppliers with parent-subsidiary relationships standardized to 54,000.

- 25,000 material groups manually assigned to 270 eCl@ss categories.

- Numerous standard reports available.

D4 Standardization

Almost since industrialization first started, industrial standards have existed in Europe and the USA for small parts such as spacers, distance sleeves, slide bearings, insulating sleeves, nuts, finishing washers, quick connectors, screws, bolts, circlips, drive fasteners and washers. So why do we see a huge increase in the use of non-standard parts?

This question is also being asked by plant managers, who face increasing difficulties in finding the space for the enormous number of containers required, each holding a different type of small part. Standardization, i.e. striving to use as many standard parts as possible is an antidote to this trend. The savings that can be realized in material costs, production, service and logistics are obvious. Ultimately, this approach matches the idea behind introducing industrial standards in the first place, namely to make life easier for engineers.

The process of standardization is easy to manage. The first step is to identify parts or groups of parts that can be replaced by standard parts. This is followed by selection of standard parts best suited for the job based on simple substitution criteria, i.e. similarities in material, material properties, dimensions and tolerances, comparability of surface coatings, and similar or enhanced functionality.

Standardization programs tend to face a number of obstacles. Here are some of the objections frequently heard:

- "Every technical change also means changes to the drawings, and that will take too much time."

- "Small parts are parts with very low costs, so it's not worth making any changes."

- "The customers don't want changes; we would have to get every single change approved by customers."

- "To implement standardization, we would have to make major changes to our processes."

The most powerful lever for overcoming these obstacles is to bundle all the standardization ideas into one big program. This usually allows a convincing volume of savings to be achieved, and hence an acceptable ROI.

Case example: Purchasing of small parts in the aviation industry

An American company makes turbines for winged aircraft and helicopters. The small parts are characterized by great diversity and small purchasing volumes. They are used both in production and as spare parts for resale to airlines and servicing firms.

There are many barriers to the purchasing of small parts in the aviation industry. Various official regulations have to be met, such as the Fastener Quality Act, FAA guidelines and Defense Department guidelines. In addition, there are internal guidelines that have to be fulfilled in the event of a change of supplier, including tests and certifications. To make matters yet more complicated, various industrial standards come into play, such as AN, AS, BAS, MS and NAS.

A brief analysis of the parts lists showed that more than 6,000 active small parts were in use, either in design and production or as spare parts. For around 70 percent of these parts, there was no corresponding industrial standard at all. Benchmarking against the leading com-

> panies in the industry revealed that only 40 percent still had specially made parts. As a result, a standardization program was launched. An interdisciplinary team made up of personnel from purchasing, engineering and quality reviewed over a thousand drawings to identify which of the specially produced parts could be replaced by standard ones.
>
> A key factor for rapid implementation of the program was use of the "Part Substitution List (PSL)", which enabled FAA requirements to be fulfilled. The outcome of the standardization process was the replacement of over 30 percent of specially made parts by standard ones. And as a result, material costs for small parts fell by 25 percent.

D5 Complexity reduction

A number of studies have demonstrated a negative correlation between a company's complexity and its earnings performance. What applies at the overarching corporate level applies equally to product complexity, and hence to interaction with suppliers.

More and more companies find themselves beset by the effects of increasing product complexity. The drivers of this development are diverse, and include the wish to meet differing customer needs, shorter product lifecycles, high innovation rates, and sometimes also a lack of discipline in development and product management. Consequently, it is virtually impossible to obtain volume-based concessions from suppliers.

When it comes to bringing product complexity under control in a systematic manner, a four-step approach has proved useful:

1. Production of variant trees: The aim is to generate transparency and help explain the complexity existing within product groups. To this end, the factors driving complexity are identified. In the case of gearboxes, for example, these factors are as follows:

    ☐ Type – Manual, automatic or double-clutch gearbox.

    ☐ Mode of installation – Lengthwise, transverse or rear engine.

    ☐ Performance range – Torque above or below 300 Nm.

    In this example, around 50 complexity drivers can be found. The existing gearboxes are then depicted in a tree structure, in accordance with their complexity drivers. The variant trees are enriched with additional data (e.g. prices of parts, quantities, warranty costs, etc.), so that a complete visualization is available by the end of the first step.

2. Creation of a maximum scenario: This involves recognizing similar variants within the variant tree and identifying potential through amalgamation or elimination.

3. Creation of a business case: In this step, the cost savings potential and income effects are compared with investment and resource requirements. A fact-based decision can then be taken on the basis of the business case.

4. Creation of an action plan: Interdisciplinary discussions are held between product management, sales, R&D, production and purchasing. Decisions are then taken with regard to detailed complexity reduction measures and the production of an implementation plan.

These measures enable purchasing to buy fewer parts with higher volumes in future. Savings are achieved not only by purchasing, thanks to better purchasing prices, but also by R&D, production and logistics.

Case example: Complexity reduction at a manufacturer of heating systems

The portfolio of bought-in hot water accumulators at a manufacturer of heating systems grew over time as the various brands of the group proliferated. Prior to a purchasing project, there was no systematic attempt or initiative to curb the diversity of products. A first-time collection of data on the purchasing group revealed 293 material numbers, with products purchased from 15 different suppliers. While that did not sound good, it did not yet allow a final judgement. Thus, the next step was to make the product groups and variants comparable with one other. With the aid of a uniform classification, a variant tree was drawn up.

On the basis of the classification and the variant tree, it was now possible to analyze prices for the first time. The very first comparisons of identically classified material numbers revealed significant price differences. The sourcing category team began by identifying variants that could be eliminated in the product range. It found, for example, that one variant had been sold to customers only eight times in a calendar year. Yet despite this low turnover, there was even a marketing leaflet available for the product. Ultimately, in consultation with marketing, a total of one third of the variants was identified as being dispensable without any loss of choice for the customers. This was accompanied by cutting the number of suppliers from 15 to 9. The resulting savings from this relatively simple and quick measure amounted to one million US dollars, not including further effects from simplified handling and reduced volume of product literature.

D6 Process benchmark

Process benchmark is best used for products characterized by numerous, relatively simple and clearly defined processes. If possible, these processes should also be available individually on the market. A good example are turned parts, where it is possible to easily switch between individual steps such as cutting, bending, turning, surface finishing, coating, etc. The best time for process benchmark is during the tendering phase for a product. Along with their normal bids, suppliers are also requested to offer detailed costs for each individual processing step (e.g. surface treatment of turned parts). Based on this information, purchasing can then negotiate directly with suppliers with regard to process costs.

The procedure for identifying savings potential by benchmarking the production processes comprises four steps:

1. Preparation for benchmarking: First, it is necessary to identify the production steps that most strongly impact the product price. At the same time, one must identify the suppliers to be invited to take part in the process benchmark. These may include both existing suppliers and new ones.

2. Involvement of the suppliers: As the next step, an invitation to tender is sent out to the already defined suppliers. The invitation includes questionnaires on the cost and time required for individual process steps.

3. Identification of best practice costs: The offers from the various suppliers are compared in detail. One first checks to see which production steps are the main cost drivers. Summing up the least expensive production steps, together with comparing external data sources,

determines the best practice process. The difference between each supplier's process costs and best practice is computed, and this determines the amount of potential savings.

4. Implementation of savings potential: Part of the savings potential is achieved directly in negotiations with suppliers. In the case of complex changes in production processes, the suppliers must submit an implementation plan.

For purchasing, the benefits of process benchmark are a high level of price transparency and fact-based decision-making. Knowing the suppliers' production processes and the costs associated with them is an aid for negotiations, which can be conducted in a more substantive and targeted manner. The database of best practice process costs created during the benchmarking procedure can also help determine future target prices for new products. A crucial factor for successful process benchmark is the involvement of production and engineering at an early stage.

Case example: Purchasing of structural components for aircrafts

In the production of passenger aircrafts, components made of composites are increasingly replacing those made of aluminum alloys. Apart from their lower weight, the big advantage of composites is the ability to produce large, complex components all in one piece, where a large number of aluminum parts would previously have been necessary. Given that aircraft manufacturers still have limited experience with this technology, one company decided to conduct process benchmark as part of tendering for structural components for a new range of aircraft. A process-benchmarking questionnaire was included in the request for a "conventional" product-price bid. Disclosure of costs for individual process steps by suppliers was a precondition for acceptance of their offers.

One of the new suppliers surprised the company with unexpectedly low costs for the process steps "cutting" and "fiber positioning". On querying these prices, it emerged that the supplier had been able to use automation to accelerate production and maximize use of material.

These prices then became the basis for comparing process costs and calculating guideline figures. The results of the procedure were put to double use in negotiations with suppliers. First, it was possible to determine new target prices on the basis of the lowest costs per process step; second, suppliers were made aware of the possibility of automating the processes of cutting and fiber positioning. The new supplier responsible for providing this information was chosen as the top partner for the future and is being awarded successively bigger orders.

D7 Design for manufacture

Design for manufacture is a systematic method for designing products so that they are easy and cheap to produce. The method consists of four steps:

- Analysis of the costs of manufacturing a product: First, all the prematerial and processing costs have to be established in detail so as to identify the major cost blocks.

- Generation of a cost driver tree: A cost driver tree is created as a means of analyzing the source of costs.

- Generation of recommendations for action: On the basis of the cost driver tree, ideas are generated for lower-cost design.

- Implementation of the new, lower-cost design: In the course of calculating the costs of the new product, the solutions with the highest savings are applied.

Application of the design for manufacture procedure highlights strengths, weaknesses and success factors in the field of design. Besides purchasing, financial controlling, production, engineering and sales, all other stakeholders should be involved right from the start, with everyone working together.

Based on the experience gained in numerous projects, five main factors have been identified for ensuring successful design for manufacture activities:

- The work must only be started when the detailed cost structure is known.

- Suppliers must be closely involved in the design for manufacture process so that their ideas can be included.

- All the departments involved must understand the needs and interests of the other departments.

- Ideas without actual relevance to cost cutting should be dropped as quickly as possible.

- The service to the customers must not be affected by cost reductions, either in perception or in scope.

> *Case example: Shift forks at a gearbox manufacturer*
>
> A gearbox manufacturer wanted to reduce costs by changing specifications. A wide range of possibilities was discussed with the supplier in the context of a workshop. At present, some production steps involve milling, and parts are sent to another of the supplier's plants in Romania for this purpose. One workshop-generated idea was to no longer produce the necessary holes by milling, but by stamping instead. It is of course impossible to achieve the same tolerances with stamping as with milling, but if the outcome is considered acceptable, cost reductions of 15 percent can be attained. After consulting with R&D, the company began producing parts with stamped holes, which were exhaustively tested and ultimately approved for series production.

D8 Specification assessment

R&D departments are continually learning. As raw material prices change, it often becomes evident that once the production processes in regular production are stabilized, smaller safety margins for tolerances are sufficient. In the development process, compromises are sometimes made under time pressure even though, on closer inspection, better solutions would have been available. In short, framework conditions change, and it therefore makes good sense to subject originally justified specifications to critical review and analysis from time to time. Specifications that are no longer necessary can be revised and adjusted in line with current needs.

An important factor in this process is complete openness towards every kind of specification change. Specification assessment is normally conducted in a workshop-like process. The workshop participants should comprise engineers, production experts, financial controllers, purchasers and suppliers. This means that all aspects of a change in the specifications can be considered right away, thus avoiding protracted iteration loops.

The analysis should begin by focusing on underlying customer requirements, since current specifications represent the original solution for meeting these requirements. Thus, the specification analysis process enquires whether these requirements could also be met by modified specifications, e.g. using another material, another thickness or different tolerances – especially in light of changing framework conditions or additional information acquired. The main focus of the analysis will naturally be on those specifications mainly responsible for driving costs. But a number of smaller changes can also lead to considerable cost savings, especially if they are easy to implement. Following the workshop, an evaluation of savings is carried out, and a business case is produced.

Case example: A gearbox manufacturer

Because of a sharp rise in extra costs for alloys on the raw materials side, material specifications were subjected to systematic review by a gearbox manufacturer. During the development phase, the material 18CrNiMo7-6 had been chosen for use in a drive shaft over the material 20MnCrS5, on account of its slightly better performance. At the time, this decision was correct and reasonable. In recent years, however, the alloy surcharge per metric ton of 18CrNiMo7-6 has risen by 500 US dollars more than for 20MnCrS5. Given a drive shaft weighing 7 kg, the use of 20MnCrS5 thus produces a cost savings of 3.5 US dollars, or 25%. The drive shaft with the alternative material was tested and approved for use.

E1 Global sourcing

Try the following: First, mark the headquarters of randomly selected major companies on a map, and then enter the locations of their active suppliers as well. This will reveal the following phenomenon: Companies situated more towards the middle of a country are more or less surrounded by a circle of suppliers. In the case of companies close to the border, the suppliers form a rough semicircle. In other words, German companies still tend to use mostly German suppliers, just as French companies continue to use mostly French suppliers. Thus, we can reasonably conclude that it is not always the best supplier for the job who actually gets the contract.

This is where global sourcing comes in: by pushing open the door to the international supplier market. The core elements of global sourcing are utilization of the worldwide supplier market and the issuance of offer-solicitation documents designed for international use.

Nowadays, identifying suppliers throughout the world has become a great deal easier thanks to the supplier directories available on the internet. Provided it is done professionally, the goal of purchasing should be no less than to identify all potential suppliers throughout the world. It is not unusual these days to send inquiries to 5,000 suppliers or more for just a single product group.

The primary language of purchasing is English. Therefore all documents used by purchasing in its interaction with suppliers must be in correct and clearly comprehensible English. This applies to image brochures as well as quotation forms, drawings, specifications, standards and business terms.

In addition to these "hard factors," the parties involved must also be open to doing business with suppliers from other cultures.

Case example: The very first global sourcing project

The global sourcing project launched by GM/Opel in the mid-1980s is both renowned and notorious. This was the first project in the world to achieve massive savings for a company through the globalization of purchasing. The success of the project was built on the following cornerstones:

- Greater attention to purchasing by the managing board

    During the project, Ignacio López, who headed the global sourcing project, was given a seat on the managing board. He was thus one of the first, if not the very first, purchasing executives to be made a member of the board of directors anywhere in the world. This sent a clear signal to all parties, both within the company and amongst suppliers, that purchasing was serious business. Purchasing subsequently acquired a completely new status, with a much stronger focus being placed on suppliers.

- Breaking traditional supplier relationships wide open

    Relationships between purchasers and suppliers, which often went back many years, were put under the spotlight. One of the most effective methods was to rotate the responsibilities of the purchasing staff. As one of the parties involved remarked at the time: "Savings of five percent could already be achieved simply by shifting the responsibility for suppliers."

- New challenge for suppliers: International competition

  In the GM/Opel global sourcing project, the international supplier market was systematically studied and addressed for the first time. For larger procurement volumes, purchasers located in the various national markets were instructed to obtain offers from their regular, local suppliers. These offers were compared with one another in a strategy known as "global competition." This approach naturally played to the professional pride and ambition of purchasers. Each one hoped that the supplier he had nominated would be victorious. The result was that negotiations between purchasers and "their" suppliers were correspondingly focused and tough.

The long-term effects of the upgrade in status of purchasing at automotive suppliers and in the European auto industry has been described as follows by one German auto executive: "No one in the industry, and especially no supplier, will openly admit that López was a good thing for all parties. But just look back at the situation in the late 1980s. The entire European industry was coming under massive pressure from Japan. The global sourcing project came just in time to make the whole industry leaner, faster, more innovative and more competitive. The fact that we, and all other European OEMs, are still in relatively good shape is largely due to the measures taken by Opel at that time. Without López's global sourcing project, the industry would be far worse off today."

E2 Make or buy

According to a rule of thumb, activities that constitute a company's core competence or that are based on a sustainable cost advantage should be performed internally.

Core competencies can be recognized on the basis of two criteria:

- First, it is necessary to ascertain whether or not a certain product or process is strategically important for the company. Strategically important products or processes are those that embody a proprietary technology or have high customer value. One way of measuring strategic importance is to determine the R&D expenditure on the product concerned.

- The second criterion is of an operative nature, namely the extent to which the company's own abilities to produce a particular product are better than those of other existing suppliers. This "operative performance" can be assessed on the basis of three factors: process reliability, service, and product quality. Important indicators in this regard are the number of (internal) complaints or the fault rate for certain products. The criterion of operative performance also measures the extent to which suppliers or production capacities are available in sufficient numbers/quantities.

Competitiveness can be assessed on the basis of two criteria as well:

- The first criterion involves evaluating the extent to which a process or product currently produced in-house is cost-efficient. This can be done by comparing the company's own cost structure with that of alternative sources. In this context, a high degree of "costing honesty" is necessary. Especially when it comes to the valuation of activities performed in-house, it frequently happens that cost-effectiveness is rated too optimistically through failure to adequately factor in overhead. This criterion also includes assessing the rate of internal capacity utilization and how, in the event of under-utilization, in-sourcing can serve as a lever.

- Besides cost-effectiveness, the second criterion for evaluating competitiveness is the extent to which the cost item can be improved. This question calls for an objective analysis of profitability. As soon as a gap is found between the in-house cost and the outsourcing possibility, an assessment is made of how the profitability gap can be closed.

Case example: Assembly of printed circuit boards

A maker of technologically advanced household appliances recognized the importance of electronics early on. Already in the 1980s, the company was one of the first to change over from electro-mechanical to fully electronic controls. This gave it an enormous image boost in the eyes of both customers and sales representatives, who serve as crucial marketing intermediaries.

Since those pioneering days, the company has maintained an extensive production capability for electronic components, at the heart of which are automatic placement machines for assembling printed circuit boards. These machines had pride of place in factory tours sponsored by the company, which were intended to impress sales representatives of the company's competence in electronics. The value of the machines was virtually never questioned.

> As part of a purchasing project, the prices for electronic components assembled by the automatic placement machines were subjected to external comparison. This revealed that the company's own component prices were often many times higher than market prices, and that the components themselves belonged to an aging generation.
>
> On closer examination, the company found that maintaining its own automatic placement machines was actually a burden. The expensive machines were working well below capacity, and were thus kept in operation roughly twice as long as those at EMS (electronic manufacturing services) specialists such as Flextronics International. The in-house electronics developers had simply accepted this situation, ignored technological advances on the international market, and designed controls that fit the existing placement machines. Purchasing, on the other hand, was left to struggle with a negligibly small number of units compared to those of EMS suppliers.
>
> Thus, a former core competence had turned into a competitive disadvantage. Given these facts, company management quickly took the necessary corrective action.

E3 Supplier market intelligence

As a strategically important department, purchasing must have thorough knowledge of the supplier market and must update this knowledge at regular intervals. Systematic supplier market intelligence is therefore one of purchasing's core tasks. Supplier market intelligence can be divided into two major areas:

- Existing suppliers: The procurement, analysis and interpretation of internal and external information on existing suppliers. Internal information should comprise not only purely cost-oriented figures (e.g. sourcing volumes, price development, etc.), but also key figures on supply capability, quality, results and innovation. Internal information should be supplemented by external data such as credit and press information. Another important aspect of supplier market intelligence is keeping an eye on the supplier market, for instance by attending trade fairs to obtain a first-hand perspective.

- New suppliers: Supplier market intelligence also has the goal of obtaining information about new suppliers. The aim is to be up to date on the latest developments on the market. External supplier market intelligence is done through the ad-hoc use of external supplier databases (e.g. http://www.alibaba.com), the creation of a web-based supplier portal and the establishment of an international sourcing office.

Regardless of whether the information is available externally or internally, an important factor in successful supplier market intelligence is the systematic gathering of supplier information, ideally in the form of a central supplier database. In this respect, purchasing can learn from marketing: By analogy with "customer relationship management" (CRM), systematic supplier market intelligence requires "supplier relationship management" (SRM). The key is that relevant information be systematically collected, entered and evaluated, so that it can be used by the responsible member of the purchasing staff.

Case example: Establishment/utilization of an international sourcing office in China

A medium-sized plant manufacturer wanted to increase the purchasing volume from China used in its European production. The reasons for this were increasing cost pressures and the fact that previous tendering processes (in which mostly West-European suppliers had taken part) had not resulted in significant extra savings. It was decided to remedy the lack of knowledge of the Chinese supplier market by setting up a local sourcing office in China.

Two years after the office was opened, the volume purchased from China was still next to nothing. An investigation of the causes revealed the following: A former project manager who had already overseen a plant opening in China had been sent to head the sourcing office. One of the stipulations he was given was that the sourcing office should be self-supporting within two years. However, due to his insufficient knowledge of the language, he was unable to use local information sources or events to identify suppliers. Moreover, there was no organizational link between the purchasing office in China and the European purchasing organization. In fact, European Purchasing hardly made any use of offers from China, merely employing them as "stick" to threaten existing suppliers. Consequently, there was no way for the anticipated cost advantages to be achieved.

After two years, the purchasing strategy in China was reviewed. The Chinese sourcing office was greatly expanded by recruiting ten local employees. In addition, the performance-related pay for engineering and purchasing personnel in Europe was tied to an increase in the volume sourced from China. Thus, after another two years, the volume purcha-

> sed from China now accounts for around 20 percent of total procurement. Cost advantages (after transport, import duties, insurance) of up to 40 percent have been realized with regard to bought-in parts.

E4 RFI/RFP process

The first step of the process is to obtain a small amount of key information from a large number of theoretically capable suppliers using RFIs (requests for information). The next step is to obtain highly detailed information from a small number of interested, qualified suppliers using RFPs (requests for proposal).

The RFI/RFP process has become part of the basic repertoire of purchasers, who have gained wide-ranging experience in its use. Nonetheless, there still seems to be room for improvement in its application.

An RFI should be as concise and simple as possible. It typically consists of three parts:

- A cover letter to introduce the inquiring company and arouse interest on the part of the supplier.

- A general section typically the same for all RFIs, requesting details about a small number of key aspects, such as sales, employee numbers and customer referrals.

- A section specifically relating to the sourcing category(s) concerned. This includes a limited number of questions that enable the inquiring company to determine whether the supplier can meet specifications and is interested in an RFP.

The main goal of the RFI is to achieve the highest response rate possible. The RFI should therefore be structured so that it can be completed by a member of the supplier's staff in a matter of minutes. As many questions as possible should be answerable simply by being checked off. One mistake frequently observed in the design of RFIs: pages and pages of questions that sometimes resemble a commercial or technical audit!

This RFI is then sent to the maximum possible number of potential suppliers of the goods in question. The list of potential suppliers should be based on a wide variety of sources and resources, e.g. databases, internet research, known suppliers. Formerly, RFIs were sent manually by fax. Today, more elegant methods are available, e.g. email or the use of professional fax services.

The RFI has two main functions. First, to obtain basic information from suppliers concerning their product range, capabilities, customer references and technologies. This data then provides a basis for selecting the suppliers to whom an RFP will be sent. Second, the RFI has a communicative function. Sending the RFI to a large number of targets communicates to a broad audience that new suppliers are being sought. This has the effect of waking up the competition at an early stage of the sourcing process. Thus, it can produce a speedy improvement in negotiating position, especially on the part of existing suppliers.

Using the RFI responses as a basis, one then selects the suppliers who will receive an RFP along with relevant technical data. In producing the RFP, care should be taken to avoid tying up suppliers' resources. Suppliers do not have an unlimited number of engineers and cost accountants at their disposal, and have to prioritize their deployment. It is therefore critical to make the RFP as supplier-friendly as possible.

A key component of the RFP process is a clearly structured proposal sheet that lists required parts, with space for the supplier to enter its prices. It is important to clearly define what price level is being requested, i.e. on what delivery terms (ex works, DDP), with or without tooling costs, etc. The proposal sheet should be easy to understand and easy to complete, and should allow simple and systematic evaluation of responses.

The proposal sheet should be accompanied by all the necessary technical information. This includes drawings for each part number, specification or data sheets, as well as generally applicable technical standards. It is essential to ensure that the supplier can clearly identify what technical information refers to which component. Ideally, data files with technical drawings should have the same name as the parts being inquired about. Unclear inquiries are one of the most common reasons suppliers discontinue preparation of an offer and turn their attention to another inquiry instead.

One should also remember to provide feedback to participating suppliers. Such feedback should be given immediately after an offer is received, and should compare the offer's terms with those of existing suppliers. This gives offering suppliers the opportunity to improve their offer right at the start. Feedback is also important in that it ensures a supplier has understood all the requirements.

Finally, feedback should also be given to all those suppliers who were not invited to negotiate. Experience has shown that feedback provided to excluded suppliers is often inadequate. One should bear in mind that preparing offers involves a great deal of time and effort. To ensure that excluded suppliers bid again in future (this time perhaps successfully), they must be given feedback as to why their offers were rejected.

Case example: Turnaround at a European-American truck maker

Around the mid-1990s, a major truck maker (with worldwide output of some 60,000 units) began thinking about sustainably improving its margins. Although the truck business was subject to strong cyclical fluctuations, some competitors were managing to stay in the black throughout the entire business cycle. This truck maker, by contrast, consistently went into the red whenever business slackened, and only managed to make a profit in years when demand was strong. Numerous discussions with external experts convinced top-management that a turnaround could be achieved with the aid of a purchasing project. It was decided that the entire procurement volume of some three billion US dollars should be made the subject of an RFI/RFP process, consisting of five "waves" lasting six months each.

In the planning phase, a management committee was set up to steer the purchasing initiative. This committee consisted of the COO, the Head of Purchasing and the Head of R&D, as well as those responsible for purchasing and R&D in key regions. Thus, the project enjoyed the full support of management. At the two main project sites, generously equipped workrooms were established where the team of in-house and external staff could collaborate full time. The relevance of the project was also underscored by additional measures:

- For the launch of Wave 1 (plus each of the other waves), all personnel involved were gathered in one place. As the two main sites were located on different continents, this involved lots of travel.

- The kick-off meeting was attended by the entire managing board. Each board member gave a presentation, highlighting the importance of the project for his/her sphere of responsibility.

- A two-day training course for participating personnel was held during each wave.

- Project teams submitted weekly progress reports to the management committee via video conferencing, whereby great weight was attached to regular attendance. The board members also took part regularly.

- In negotiations with major suppliers, the board took on operative project tasks and cooperated smoothly with the responsible project teams.

For Wave 1, ten sourcing categories – Outer Skin, Injection Systems, Tires, Semi-Trailers, Forgings, Bearings, Brakes, Air-conditioning/Heating, Pneumatics and Pressings – were selected and assigned to three project teams. Along with two project leaders, one team leader and two to three team members were assigned to each team. Altogether, the project comprised eleven to thirteen full-time employees of the truck maker.

RFIs were sent to a total of 1,643 existing and new suppliers, mostly in Europe and North America. In line with the technology of the time, this meant dialing numbers on fax machines. A total of 671 responses were received from suppliers.

The next step was to prepare the RFPs. Drawings and specifications were copied. An entire series of mini-production lines was set up for compiling the RFPs. Stacks of drawings and specifications were lined up side by side in long corridors. Team members walked along the rows, making up RFP packages for the suppliers. At that time, the term "RFP package" still indicated an actual physical object, with the packages being sent out in large cardboard boxes.

> No fewer than 429 RFPs were dispatched in this way. Of these, 370 elicited responses. During Wave 1, the whole team achieved savings of twelve percent on a volume of 350 million US dollars. Around two-thirds of these savings were a direct result of negotiations with existing suppliers. The remaining third required a change of suppliers, and hence an approval process for the specific sourcing categories concerned.
>
> In view of the great success of Wave 1, management decided to broaden the project. Thanks to the savings achieved in Waves 1 to 5 using the tools of the RFI/RFP process, the truck maker advanced from being one of the weakest players in the industry to a solid, mid-level competitor.

E5 Visible process organization (VPO)

The past decade has seen a great deal of M&A activity in many industries. The large new companies that have resulted appear to fulfill many of the success factors postulated in the mid-1990s, e.g. global presence, comprehensive product and brand portfolios, and especially critical mass. Nevertheless, the conglomerates created through these mergers and acquisitions are often less profitable than smaller niche players. How come?

One reason is that niche players have simple decision-making structures and usually know their customers well. Large groups of companies, on the other hand, have complex hierarchies and have to meet a wide range of customer needs using intricate internal and external production networks.

In response, many large companies have taken steps to improve their synergy potential. In the pharmaceutical industry for instance, a number of firms have used M&As to replenish their product pipelines and thus boost competitiveness. Through the use of platform and shared-part strategies, the auto industry has succeeded in standardizing those parts that are not visible to end-customers, across product lines and even across brands. These measures allow product development times to be significantly reduced, while model variety can be increased.

Thus, determined efforts are being made to tackle technical complexity by means of standardization. However, reduced technical complexity leads directly to an increase in management complexity: In a company with several divisions already using shared parts, it becomes difficult to coordinate market demand with the production resources installed at the company's own plants and at suppliers. This coordination has to take place not only among the functions for a given division (purchasing, production, and sales/marketing), but also among all the divisions within a single function. Unless this is done successfully, one cannot ensure, for instance, that the purchasing departments of all the functions involved are able to forward useful demand information to a shared supplier.

Managers regularly complain that coordinating market demand with production resources within the group works poorly in practice. As a rule, planning processes are sequentially structured, and seek to produce a precise and sustainable plan for departmental silos for the coming planning period (typically from two to six months). The sub-plans created by the departments and divisions involved are only aggregated once during the entire planning period. If events occur during the period that run counter to plan, the corporate culture often causes them to be ignored until it is too late.

Having to admit that a plan needs to be changed is seen as a personal failure by many. Thus, departments often stick to their plan, despite obvious deficiencies, until the discrepancies become so great that the entire plan must be scrapped. By then, however, the decision backlog has become so long that no single department is able to affect a solution. The outcome is that a problematic package is escalated to group top-management. Due to lack of detailed knowledge, however, the group's top-management may also be unable to find a decision beneficial to the business as a whole.

Visible process organization (VPO) is an innovative model that can turn the black box of "operations" into an efficient and effective organization whose processes are transparent and whose decisions can be taken in real time. Thus, it enables the company to respond quickly and effectively to changes in customer demand, in the supplier market or in the competitive environment as a whole. Visible process organizations are closely modeled on the Mission Control Center of NASA. After a detailed study of the Johnson Space Center in Houston, a team of A.T. Kearney consultants identified the following success factors for NASA process management:

- Permanent deployment of decision makers in one place: From lift-off in Cape Canaveral all the way to landing, space missions are managed by the Mission Control Center. The Mission Control Center itself is manned with one representative for each of the critical disciplines, e.g. Propulsion, Navigation, Systems, Payload and Communications. Each Mission Controller in turn is just the "tip of an iceberg," and is backed up by support teams of up to 1,000 staff.

- Dynamic re-planning process: NASA process management is designed to continuously monitor complex data streams for unforeseen events. If such events occur, they are immediately evaluated by the Mission Control team in terms of import and urgency. If need be, adjustments are made to the plan. As NASA puts it: "We are not in the planning business – we are in the re-planning business."

- Rule-based decisions: Clear, pragmatic decision-making rules are in place for handling the most critical situations. These rules ensure that the Mission Control Center focuses on solutions when under time pressure, rather than engaging in abstract discussions.

- Delegation of decision-making powers to the Mission Control team: NASA's top-management delegates full decision-making competence for a mission to the Control Center. Any subsequent intervention will be in accordance with the decision-making rules.

Based on A.T. Kearney's experience, the following are critical success factors for the introduction of VPO:

- Focus and commitment by top-management.

- Selection of the VPO team.

- Concomitant change management.

The introduction of VPO will inevitably engender resistance within a company. VPO can be misunderstood as a centralistic approach. Particular departments may shun the transparency associated with VPO. Employees may refuse to move their office or to work in the open-office atmosphere of a VPO room. All these reservations can cause a VPO project to founder. It is therefore crucial to obtain total commitment from the group's top-management even before the project begins. Unity among the group's top-management will keep the project's launch on course even during critical phases.

The group's top-management needs to be aware that they are setting a milestone for the entire industry by opting for VPO. As a member of a major automotive group's management put it: "VPO will be the defining organizational structure for the group during the next ten years. It will assist us in translating the benefits of our platform and shared-parts strategy into corporate success."

The selection of the VPO team is of key importance. Besides their professional expertise, ideal candidates should be highly regarded within their regular work spheres and have strong team-working skills. Especially the selection of initial team members should be done under the supervision of experienced HR experts. Appointment to the team should be seen as a unique distinction within the company and as a positive career move.

Change management for the introduction of VPO should be supported by specialists with experience in both the organization and operation of mission control centers in space travel or similar fields. This will ensure that the VPO team can continually refer to the relevant benchmarks when defining modes of operation. In fact, A.T. Kearney sometimes enlists the services of NASA experts in its VPO projects.

Case example: Automaker

Contrary to an automaker's plan, the demand for diesel cars turned out to be far greater than anticipated, and suppliers were unable to deliver enough injection pumps. The board therefore decided to undertake sales promotion to at least maintain the current turnover on markets that prefer gasoline-powered cars (North America). These measures proved successful, and demand in the US actually increased. However, the proportion of vehicles ordered with air-conditioning was significantly higher in the US than in Germany. In addition to the shortage of diesel engines, there was now also a shortfall in A/C units. These homemade bottlenecks meant that even moderate fluctuations in market demand had a serious impact on the automaker. The amplitude of demand fluctuation increased further along the supply chain in the direction of suppliers, until all that the latter received was a kind of meaningless "background noise." As a result, suppliers were forced to maintain a high safety margin in their stocks in order to deliver on time.

The visible process organization (VPO) devised by A.T. Kearney, with its ability to take rapid decisions based on real-time information, allowed the level of stocks and inventories (along with the capital they represent) to be substantially reduced. At the same time, VPO helped avoid bottlenecks and led to higher sales. As soon as the VPO team learned that demand for diesel engines was rising, for example, it could pass this information on to procurement, production and logistics, as well as to suppliers. The introduction of VPO therefore allowed the automaker to solve its homemade problems once and for all, saving two billion euros per year in uncertainty costs.

E6 Collaborative capacity management

Capacity management was an important topic in production even when machine utilization was still managed by card systems. Today, internet applications are available to handle capacity management between companies and external suppliers, with the ability to support all relevant processes over time and for a broad range of parts.

Collaborative capacity management enables continuous communication and collaboration among suppliers, purchasing and logistics. The key elements of collaborative capacity management are as follows:

- Internet-based communication of demand and capacities.
- Assurance of critical capacities and simulation of production-program scenarios.
- Integration of the supplier into the program-planning process.

Purchasing breaks down planned demand for a given period (usually six months) into smaller segments (usually several weeks) and loads this data onto the internet platform, usually updating it weekly. The suppliers upload their planned capacities onto the internet platform as well. A program (also located on the internet platform) then compares planning demand with planning capacities. If deviations are limited to a certain bandwidth, the program performs its own reconciliation. If deviations occur in excess of the bandwidth, the program calls for manual intervention.

The early detection of potential bottlenecks reduces bottleneck costs such as special trips and increased parts costs, while also avoiding process costs on the part of the OEM and the supplier.

Case example: Collaborative capacity management via the internet in the automotive industry

A German automaker created a collaborative capacity management system using an internet platform. One critical factor proved to be choosing appropriate parts based on a parts selection strategy, since it is naturally impossible to keep track of all parts using a system of this kind. The automaker's system ultimately focused on 1,500 parts that were used across brands, especially assemblies and gearboxes. In any one calendar year, these products alone gave rise to bottleneck costs of some 50 million US dollars.

> This capacity management system brought about major changes within the company. The system's targeted introduction within the company and at suppliers was supported by a change management project consisting of the following:
>
> - Building understanding and acceptance within the organization.
> - Moderation and resolution of problem fields at external suppliers.
> - Ensuring utilization by purchasers.
> - Proactive identification and avoidance of "pitfalls" during use.
> - Proactive support and targeted development of improvements within a user group (internal users and suppliers).
>
> The system allowed impending bottlenecks to be recognized and dealt with more quickly. Following introduction of the system, bottleneck costs for the parts in question were reduced by up to 50 percent.

E7 Supplier tiering

At any company, there are meaningful scopes of management responsibility that should not be exceeded. Dividing responsibility over a corresponding number of tiers allows even very large firms (100,000 employees and more) to be managed efficiently. Many companies also apply a similar tiering principle to managing suppliers.

Supplier tiering originated in the auto industry and can be best understood in the context of automakers' changing priorities over the last 40 years:

- 1970s – The typical automaker was still characterized by strong vertical integration, making practically all key vehicle components itself.

- 1980s – Under the pressure of recession and the oil crisis, automakers sought to reduce volume risk and embarked on large-scale outsourcing of parts production to external suppliers.

- 1990s – The large number of suppliers – some automakers had 2,000 or more – became almost unmanageable. Supplier tiering was therefore introduced, whereby automakers deliberately assigned responsibility for modules and systems to so-called "1st tier suppliers." The latter acted as integrators, with the task of managing 2nd tier suppliers and improving quality and efficiency.

For purchasing, supplier tiering means finding the best structure in each particular case. In situations with a highly complex supplier landscape, it makes sense to follow the same path as the auto industry. On average, 20 percent of suppliers are responsible for 80 percent of sourcing volume. Thus, an initial solution may be to make these 20 percent 1st tier suppliers.

However, it is also possible to go the other way by actively managing 2nd tier suppliers of major modules or systems.

Case example: Purchasing driver's seats for trucks

In a purchasing project at an international truck manufacturer, seats formed an important sourcing category. Purchasing passenger seats was generally a simple matter. In the case of the driver's seats, however, there were major differences in requirements. In North America, driver's seats could be sourced relatively freely. In Europe, on the other hand, there was strong customer demand for driver's seats from one particular supplier, which accounted for a share of over 90 percent.

The construction of driver's seats for trucks is far more complex than for cars. Truck driver's seats are equipped with sophisticated shock absorbers that resemble those on the truck chassis itself. Truck drivers spend almost their entire working lives on these seats. To protect them as much as possible from occupational ailments such as damaged bones and joints, driver's seats are made to the highest safety standards.

But let us return to the supplier with the 90 percent market share. Even after intense consultation with the marketing department, it appeared virtually impossible to reduce this percentage. In order to break the impasse, the truck maker set about tearing down the supplier's seats into their constituent parts and asked the supplier for component prices. Besides seats, the purchasing project also focused on shock absorbers. Thus, one obvious step was to integrate the seat supplier's sourcing volumes for these products with those of the truck maker. Bundling this demand with the much greater volume of the truck manufacturer worked miracles: The prices offered for driver's seat shock absorbers were up to 80 percent lower than those charged previously.

This savings potential was also interesting for the seat manufacturer, since it could be applied not only to seats made for the European-American truck maker, but to practically all seats produced. In return for this and other savings proposals, the seat manufacturer granted a substantial price cut. The outcome of the project was that the truck maker could continue to use the preferred driver's seats, but at a significantly lower price – one with which the supplier was also still happy.

E8 Value chain reconfiguration

Lego bricks have fascinated generations of children. The wonderful thing about them is that the same bricks can be used to build new things. Reconfiguring the value-creation chain works along the same lines. The aim is to create flexible, intra-company structures to fulfill specific customer needs along the entire value-creation chain, from raw materials all the way to the end-consumer.

Reconfiguring the value chain involves seven steps:

1. Defining and weighting the drivers of customer value and growth.

2. Setting up a detailed value chain for the company.

3. Identifying the dependencies of the customer-value drivers, and allocating them to the segments of the value chain.

4. Allocating costs to the value chain.

5. Breaking down the value chain into core and non-core activities.

6. Screening various options: performing certain steps internally or outsourcing, omitting or leapfrogging them, and/or networking more closely with suppliers.

7. Choosing the best options and implementing them.

Using this approach, one sometimes finds that major technological advances enable key steps in the traditional value chain to be re-designed or dispensed with altogether. Examples are Dell's simplification of computer sales through configuration by customers, or online selling by amazon.com, which has revolutionized the book trade. In some cases, consumers are no longer prepared to pay for process steps that they can do themselves. Additionally, reduced transport costs and shorter transport times are increasing flexibility in the way companies produce and sell products and services throughout the world.

The goal of value chain reconfiguration is to acquire or maintain maximum control over key steps and processes, thus internalizing core competencies as a competitive advantage. At the same time, the aim is to have the least possible ownership of capital or assets involved in the value chain.

> *Case example: The consumer goods industry*
>
> Particularly in the consumer goods sector, new combinations of value steps that were once strictly separated between supplier and customer create countless opportunities for attractive new offerings, giving the customer more than just a product at the right time. A good example is the collaboration between US white goods manufacturer Whirlpool and Procter & Gamble. Whirlpool had realized that customers were tired of having to take their clothes out for dry cleaning and pressing and paying high prices. Thus, a technical solution was developed: a closet that makes clothes fresh and wrinkle-free while still on the hanger. Without a partner to supply the appropriate agents for cleaning and deodorizing, the idea was only half-baked, however. So a partnership was established with P&G, and the two companies jointly enhanced the product further until it was market-ready. Naturally, success is never guaranteed, even with an ingenious idea and a synergy of two companies' talents. One thing is certain, however: when two firms team up in their area of competency to create real customer value, the market is sure to reward them.

F1 LCC sourcing

"We want to become Number 1 in all sectors, everywhere in the world!" This seems to be the general goal in China today. Starting with raw materials and semi-finished goods, China is now building efficient industrial infrastructures all along the value chain. In many areas, however, the production capacities in place already exceed domestic demand. Many companies that invested in China hoping for a market of over a billion consumers have had to learn this the hard way.

One strategy a company can use to benefit from China's growth is LCC (low cost country) sourcing. On average, manufacturing costs in China are 50 percent lower than in Western Europe. (In fact, China is only the most prominent example of a whole series of important low-cost countries, such as Brazil, Russia, India or Turkey.) However, anyone wanting to enter into serious collaboration with Chinese suppliers must overcome a number of barriers:

- Being able to offer attractive volumes.
- Identifying interested and qualified suppliers.
- Identifying appropriate price levels.
- Establishing a robust relationship at top-management level.
- Overcoming internal resistance.
- Managing operations and risks.
- Overcoming cultural barriers.

The Chinese supplier market cannot be conquered with cautious test inquiries. Chinese companies are operating on a domestic market growing at double-digit rates every year. Potential European or American customers must offer genuinely attractive volumes that stoke the imagination of the Chinese entrepreneurs. Thus, when making inquiries, one should always offer attractively large volumes.

Identifying interesting and qualified suppliers in China is challenging. Chinese firms are bombarded day-in, day-out with inquiries from Europe and the USA. It is therefore essential to stand out in the crowd. One promising approach is to make initial contact with written documents in Mandarin, immediately followed up on the telephone by a native speaker.

As soon as offers have been received, a process of intense negotiation will set in. The first offers from China are usually not far below European or American price levels. From the Chinese point of view, the mirror image of LCC sourcing is "selling to Europe at European price levels."

Once a price level has been found that is acceptable for both sides, the next step is for top-management to take a trip to China. Chinese entrepreneurs want to actually see their counterparts. The establishment of a trusting and robust relationship is the best guarantee for overcoming all subsequent hurdles.

The first obstacle that has to be overcome is an internal one. Internal users at the European or American company back home have to be convinced of the validity of the Chinese offer. Here, a great deal of imaginative thinking may be necessary.

For managing operations, there is no practical alternative to establishing a purchasing office in China. Someone has to be present on the ground at the Chinese supplier to ensure that quality standards are complied with and (for instance) that worn-out tools are replaced. In the first few months of production startup, an almost daily presence may be required, though this can later be reduced to a weekly rhythm.

The final hurdles are cultural barriers. Genuinely close collaboration with Chinese suppliers will ultimately result in the European or American company becoming slightly more "Chinese," while the Chinese supplier adopts something of the culture of its customers.

Case example: Chinese plastic film supplier

In the course of a purchasing project, the COO of a packaging producer headed a delegation visiting attractive potential suppliers in China. For most of the delegation, this was their first professional trip to the "Middle Kingdom." After visits to a number of suppliers of paper and printing inks, the mood of initial skepticism turned into one of amazement.

The group first visited a paper factory located in a well-tended park on the banks of the Yangtze. The factory's environmental concept was unmatched anywhere else in the world. The entire logistics of the factory were handled on the river so as to keep the nearby city free of heavy goods traffic. The effluent from the factory was so clean that it could be fed into the goldfish ponds in the park. An entire R&D department was dedicated to managing the upriver wood plantations as ecologically as possible.

A tour of one of the main plants of a leading Chinese supplier of plastic films was equally impressive. The production shops were bigger than those at any comparable producer in Europe. The machines more modern and the quality perfect. At the inevitable dinner with the host's top-management, the COO mentioned a film technology that was completely new in Europe. The managing director responded that this technology was already in use by the Chinese company, though at a different plant located some 90 minutes' drive away. As the delegation's schedule for the next day was already booked with visits to other suppliers, the managing director promptly ordered three limousines and insisted on accompanying the European delegation on a visit to the other plant. The group arrived shortly after midnight, and was welcomed by the plant manager, who had been roused from bed and now took them on a tour of the plant.

On the drive back to the hotel, the COO was silent for a long time. Then he said what was on his mind: "What I've seen here in terms of equipment and product quality is better in every respect than anything the best European suppliers can offer. The prices are unbeatable. But what really won me over is the business-minded attitude of the management team. What European supplier would spontaneously set off with me on a three-hour drive to visit a plant in the middle of the night?"

It will come as no surprise that this visit laid the foundations for close and successful cooperation with the Chinese plastic-film supplier.

F2 Best shoring

The expression "IT off-shoring", i.e. the outsourcing of processes to other (geographically remote) regions first arose in connection with the large-scale outsourcing of programming and software activities to low-cost software firms in India in response to the Y2K computer threat. Among the main drivers for off-shoring were the cost advantages in India along with educational levels comparable to those in the West.

The initial hype was soon followed by disillusionment, however: outsourcing turned out to be more expensive than anticipated, time schedules were not met, cooperation proved difficult, and many companies were dissatisfied with the results. The reason for this failure was the one-dimensional nature of the outsourcing decision, which was based solely on costs and failed to account for other factors such as productivity, quality levels, operating risks, manpower availability and cultural issues.

The best-shoring strategy involves a comprehensive evaluation of which region or country a certain good or service should be produced in. Basically, there are three different types of best shoring: "On-shore" is production of the good or service in the home region, where cost structures are similar. From the European point of view, "onshore" would mean Western European countries or, from the North American point of view, Canada and the USA. The second option is "near-shore." This means manufacturing a product in a region that is geographically and culturally close but offers major cost advantages. From the Western European point of view, this would especially include Eastern Europe and Turkey, and from a North American point of view, Mexico in particular. Finally, there is "off-shore", i.e. the production of goods or services in a region that is geographically distant. Traditional off-shoring countries are India, China, Malaysia and the Philippines.

The best-shoring evaluation process selects the most favorable location by applying a comprehensive set of criteria, which include not only current cost effectiveness and scenario analyses, but also an assessment of service and quality levels, as well as the question of warranty:

- The cost effectiveness analysis should encompass detailed consideration of all relevant personnel costs. Apart from wages/salaries and payroll deductions, one should also factor in costs associated with the availability of qualified personnel, productivity issues, and possible wage increases. Many companies which shifted production processes to Eastern Europe underestimated the rate of subsequent pay increases, which in some regions were in the double-digits. Experience has shown that cost-effectiveness analyses tend to lowball the expenses involved in managing resources in the new region, as well as transaction costs for know-how transfer and training.

- Besides cost effectiveness, it is also critical to evaluate service and quality. Managing service and quality is difficult over great distances and across cultural divides. Moreover, even in India, skilled personnel are by now in short supply.

- A further aspect of evaluating locations is the possibility of making warranty claims. Warranty claims are virtually unknown in some low-cost countries. For some industries, moreover, damage or compensation claims can threaten the very survival of the business. Thus, the issue of warranty claims must be taken seriously.

- Finally, the best-shoring strategy also includes analysis and assessment of potential risks: difficult, emotionally fraught know-how transfer, high levels of personnel fluctuation, political instability, and the dangers of bundling risk at one location.

Case example: Relocation of a major German bank's graphics and editing unit

A major bank produced large quantities of German-language publications, e.g. advertising literature, employee newsletters, analyst reports, and customer presentations. Graphic processing and language editing was done by a single graphics and editing unit located in downtown Frankfurt and consisting of over 50 employees. In the context of reviewing this organization's core competencies, the question was asked whether these services should be assigned to external service providers, and whether factor cost advantages in other countries could be utilized. Since graphics processing and editing were not part of the bank's strategic core activities, and since there were a large number of firms providing such services, it was decided at a relatively early stage to outsource these activities. In order to realize the maximum savings, a further assessment was done to determine which country these services should be outsourced to, from the standpoint of cost and quality. India, which was especially popular for IT services, was not a suitable candidate. While the country was attractive for low factor costs and generally high skill levels, it lacked sufficient personnel with the specific qualifications required. After all, the graphics and editing services to be provided involved German-language publications. At that time, there were not many Indians available with perfect knowledge of the German language. For this reason, India was rejected.

In the end, the bank opted for a provider in the Czech Republic, i.e. a near-shore solution. While the level of manpower costs was not as low as in India, the country had lots of personnel with very good German language skills. By outsourcing this unit to the neighboring Czech Republic, total costs were almost halved.

F3 Reverse auctions

Since the creation of eBay, internet auctions have become the norm, even for private users. This can also be observed in sourcing, where reverse auctions have been a regular feature for years whenever the goal is to obtain simultaneous offers from several suppliers in a secure environment. Reverse auctions are a way of creating markets with significantly shorter handling times for buyers.

Before holding a reverse auction, there are four main decisions that have to be taken:

1. At what time during the offer-solicitation process will the auction be held? One possibility is for a reverse auction to be held once initial negotiations have taken place with selected suppliers. However, an auction of this kind can also be used to identify possible suppliers in the first place. Timing plays an important role because an auction can shorten the entire tendering process.

2. How many suppliers are to be included in the auction? If the primary objective is speedy completion of the tendering process, experience has shown that the auction should include 20 suppliers at most. However, if the purpose is to obtain greater insight into suppliers' pricing structures, more than 20 suppliers can be included.

3. What will the pricing structure be? If it is intended to procure a large number of individual items via the reverse auction, pricing should relate to a whole basket of products. Where only a smaller number of items are involved, it is recommended to ask for individual bids and pricing offers.

4. Finally, how long should the auction last? A meaningful auction cannot take place in less than 30 minutes. If it lasts more than two hours, on the other hand, spells of inactivity will dominate. The duration of the auction must therefore be set and adhered to on an individual basis, depending on the number of items to be procured, the price structure, and the simplicity/complexity of specifications.

The auction should relate to clearly specified product groups, so that misunderstandings can be largely ruled out. But even the best auction cannot work without open-minded and internet-friendly suppliers.

Case example: Reverse auctions by an automaker

A leading international automaker sought to achieve sustainable leadership in purchasing. One way to achieve this was the use of reverse auctions. To soften internal and external resistance, the company initiated a learning-by-doing process.

Purchasers were provided with first-rate tools for holding reverse auctions, but were not placed under pressure to use them. Ultimately, it was realized that reverse auctions are no more and no less than a means to speed up negotiations. To date, around 1,300 reverse auctions have been conducted by the automaker, accounting for a procurement volume of 17 billion US dollars.

F4 Expressive bidding

In the traditional tendering process, suppliers are only able to decide on two variables: First, whether to submit an offer or not; second, what product price to offer. However, the world is not that black-and-white. Suppliers are often prepared to make price concessions if they know they will be given a bigger slice of the pie.

Cases like this can be described as an "if-then" condition. Here is an example: "If" a supplier is awarded Part B in addition to Part A, "then" he will reduce the price for Part A by a further ten percent. Provided only a small number of total offers contain "if-then" conditions, it is easy to consider them during the evaluation process.

But as soon as offers contain a large number of "if-then" conditions, evaluation becomes more difficult, especially if such offers are submitted by suppliers bidding for different segments of the total volume available. In the face of a large number of "if-then" offers and a large number of bidding suppliers, it is almost impossible to identify the maximum possible savings using conventional means.

Expressive bidding is a strategy that allows price bids with "if-then" conditions to be submitted. On completion of the bidding process, an algorithm integrated into the expressive-bidding tool calculates the maximum possible savings at the press of a button. By changing the framework conditions or by specifying individual suppliers, purchasing can then calculate savings for various scenarios. For suppliers, expressive bidding offers lots of flexibility and opportunities for differentiation. For the purchasing company, it enables cost-cutting potential to be fully exploited.

> *Case example: Freight-transport purchasing*
>
> Purchasing freight capacities is a traditional field of application for expressive bidding. Many companies have to cover thousands of routes in distributing their goods. At the same time, the freight transport market is still highly fragmented and competitive. Freight forwarders tend to have strong regional preferences on the basis of the networks they deal with.
>
> Expressive bidding is a way of managing this supply-side complexity. During the creation of scenarios, a step-by-step procedure will often emerge, as in the following example:
>
> - 67 freight forwarders have submitted bids, including 51 that offer savings.
> - Maximum savings volume amounts to 9.2 million US dollars and would require use of 45 freight forwarders.
> - By restricting the number of active freight forwarders to 30, one could reduce savings to 6.9 million US dollars.
>
> Using this approach, savings of between 10 and 20 percent can usually be achieved.

F5 Vendor managed inventory (VMI)

There are many cases where it is not important for companies to have responsibility for stocks of materials or pre-products themselves. Inventory management is therefore entrusted to the supplier, who usually handles it on the basis of electronically transmitted consumption data. As long as regular supply entails logistical problems, this is a partnership solution that substantially reduces storage costs, while giving the supplier the advantage of strong customer loyalty. The supplier has greater freedom in planning deliveries and can thus produce in more economical batch sizes, while responding more rapidly to demand fluctuations. VMI also makes for better utilization of transport capacities, fewer emergency deliveries and reduced response times. Vendor managed inventories often take the form of consignment stocks as far as transfer of title is concerned. The stocks remain the property of the supplier until actually requisitioned for use. VMI arrangements are especially suited for merchandise stocks with predictable, relatively high consumption rates.

Moreover, mutual trust between the customer and vendor is a critical success factor for a vendor managed inventory system. Any company intending to introduce it should do so in seven steps:

- Define the parameters: The more carefully parameters are defined for each situation, the more successful the implementation of VMI (safety-buffer stock, minimum size of delivery batch, etc.).

- Specify prices for vendor managed inventories: VMI pricing must reflect the true costs to the supplier. This also indirectly determines the value of financial benefits.

- Exploit an opportunity for supplier consolidation, since greater volumes with one supplier are more likely to produce meaningful VMI arrangements.

- Share responsibility for designing the process: A VMI model requires close cooperation and complete disclosure of information by both sides.

- Introduce key performance indicators (KPI): These indicators will promote cost reductions in spite of high service levels (e.g. forecasting accuracy, warehousing bottlenecks, etc.).

- Introduce a forecasting model: Introduce a forecasting model based on historical data that factors in seasonal and other influences.

- Buyback of stocks: To start a program of vendor managed inventories, the supplier should buy up all existing stocks.

In summary: VMI arrangements work so well because they identify those cost drivers along the value-creation/supply chain that influence inventories, allowing prices to the customer to be reduced without a loss of savings by the supplier.

Case example: P&G reduces its stocks of "Pampers"

Goods consumed regularly are the ones best suited for close partnerships. Supermarkets throughout the world offer the popular "Pampers" brand of diapers. Faster product turnover means increased profit for all parties along the value chain. The principle is simple and was introduced in 1988 by WalMart in its cooperation with P&G. First, the two companies swapped quality managers so as to study the other's working conditions. They then looked for the right steps to increase sales and profits for both companies. Naturally, the topic of inventories was also considered. Granting P&G full access to WalMart's consumption and inventory data was a solution that enabled both sides to reduce their stocks. All this was done with the aid of production planning and quality management, with an eye on the just-in-time solutions of the auto industry. From the start, decisions were taken not at operating management level, but at boardroom level. As a result, P&G forecast company savings of one billion dollars in the US for the first year alone, along with comparable savings for retail customers. What was unique about this strategy (which is still in use today) was that for the first time P&G viewed retailers as its customer. In other words, it broadened its usual definition of "customer" to cover not just the end consumer of its products.

F6 Virtual inventory management

Excellent inventory management is a precondition for capacity management. It is therefore essential for a company to have its own inventories and those of its suppliers fully under control. This will largely depend on efficient IT systems. Incompatibility of systems between locations has a negative impact on inventories because the available information is inadequate. And yet it is vital to have timely knowledge about all stocks in order to optimize them to the benefit of the company and its suppliers. If existing systems do not supply integrated stock data, alternative solutions will be necessary, e.g. via an internet-based platform. These should provide integrated inventory information for at least the most important items.

What is important is that the production plant has access to its own receiving warehouses and, if need be, its own central warehouse as well. It must also be able to monitor the following: stocks at company-owned plants that are managed by suppliers; stocks at suppliers' delivery warehouses, as well as "rolling inventories" (i.e. all goods in transit by road, rail, air or water and not currently in any warehouse.)

The goal of perfect inventory management is to minimize "unofficial" safety-buffer stocks, which have a negative impact on current assets. At the same time, production losses and the resulting disruption to production must be prevented.

Knowledge of complete inventory levels enables various stock drivers to be optimized, e.g. by avoiding excessive safety-buffer stocks, and identifying little-used articles.

Case example: Steel company

A steel company's blast furnace has to operate right round the clock. It is therefore critical that deliveries of iron ore, scrap and coke unfold smoothly, thus ensuring a sufficient supply of pre-materials at all times. Given dramatic increases in the price of pre-materials, it makes sense for the steel company to further optimize its logistics chain in order to reduce inventories in transit. Thus, all pre-materials en route to the blast furnace by ship or rail anywhere in the world are recorded and tracked by an internet-based system, enabling stocks in transit to be optimized.

F7 Sustainability management

"Some of our customers have started buying our products on the basis of our commitment to sustainability!" Are these better-informed consumers, who bother to consider the sustainability of the value-creation chain, or are they idealists in pursuit of a "green" vision, without regard for economic realities?

Sustainability management strives for economic, ecological and social sustainability at one and the same time. Summed up by the motto "go green, get sustainable and be ethical," sustainability management stands for long-term thinking and action, as well as respect for ecological and ethical values. The goal of sustainability management is to preserve or create an environment fit for the next generation to live in. As this becomes a much-debated issue all over the world, more and more companies are trumpeting their commitment to sustainability. Some do so because their management is genuinely convinced that economy and ecology need not be incompatible opposites. The recent surge in the price of raw materials has certainly made careful husbanding of resources a hot-button topic. In other cases, however, sustainability claims are nothing more than a response to public pressure.

Serious sustainability management is ultimately more than just saving energy. It begins right at the start of the value-creation chain and requires companies to ensure that parts bought from suppliers have been produced in an ecologically compatible, socially acceptable manner. "Ecological compatibility" means that no harmful substances are used in production, and the environment of the supplier country is left undamaged. "Social acceptability" means, for instance, that no child labor is used and that unreasonable working conditions are avoided. Increasing numbers of companies are demanding that these criteria be met by their suppliers. It is important in this context that customers do not simply rely on information provided by a supplier, but that they carry out their own, periodic inspections on the ground.

Sustainability management prevents the occurrence of supply bottlenecks as a result of statutory restrictions on certain materials. In the process, it also prevents harm to the company's image and forestalls purchasing boycotts by consumers. Leading companies are already using sustainability management to save money through deployment of new materials or more efficient use of resources. Thus, sustainability management can even become a source of innovation.

Case example: Sustainable coffee consumption at Starbucks

In 2005, Starbucks bought 250 million lbs of green raw coffee in 27 countries (two percent of world output). Many of the coffee beans roasted by Starbucks are grown in Guatemala and Costa Rica. However, Starbucks also has good trade relations with other countries of Latin America (Mexico, El Salvador, Honduras, Panama, Colombia, Venezuela, Ecuador, Bolivia, Brazil and Peru). As a leading worldwide supplier, roaster and seller of specialty coffees, Starbucks pursues a holistic approach to sustainable coffee trading, based on six principles:

1. Starbucks pays premium prices for its coffee, thus enabling coffee growers and their families to earn an adequate living. On average, Starbucks pays 1.84 US dollars per pound of green raw coffee – 23 percent more than the world market price.

2. Starbucks ties its growers according to the coffee purchasing guidelines known as "Coffee And Farmers Equity (C.A.F.E.) Practices." This program was created in 2001 on the initiative of Starbucks with the assistance of NGOs, scientists, governments, and the coffee industry. Its goal is to ensure that high-quality coffee is grown and processed in an environmentally compatible, socially acceptable manner all along the value-creation chain.

3. In 2004, Starbucks founded the Farmer Support Center, where a team of experts investigates soil quality, crop management, coffee quality and sustainability, working closely with farmers and suppliers in Central and South America.

4. Starbucks buys coffees certified as organic by independent third parties such as Fair Trade or Shade Grown.

5. Starbucks invests in social programs designed to benefit regional coffee-farming communities.

6. Starbucks helps coffee growers gain access to affordable credit.

F8 Revenue sharing

Revenue sharing means allowing the supplier to share in business opportunities and risks. The basic precondition is that the supplier must indeed play a significant role in the success or failure of the business. As the sales revenue of a product is a clearly defined factor, it provides a solid basis for the partnership between customer and supplier.

Either the customer or the supplier may strive for revenue sharing, though with different goals in each case. If the initiative is taken by the customer, the supplier will have especially attractive products and services that the customer wishes to obtain exclusively for itself. If the initiative is taken by the supplier, the supplier's products and services will be at the start of the product lifecycle, whereby it is intended that the customer should act as a multiplier in establishing new sales channels.

> *Case example: Apple iPhone helps AT&T*
>
> Close collaboration in the value chain can easily produce a win-win situation for both companies. This was the case with the Apple iPhone: Working in close consultation with mobile telephony provider AT&T, Apple set up an arrangement that increased the sales revenue of both firms. Apple now shares in the profits from each phone call made by iPhone customers, since AT&T's revenue is boosted by the popularity of the Apple brand. The arrangement provides for Apple to receive x percent of the sales revenue produced by an iPhone, while AT&T receives (100-x) percent. This is a fair and meaningful solution for both sides. In the eyes of younger consumers, AT&T becomes associated with a product icon. Apple, for its part, earns higher sales revenue by focusing on one provider, while benefiting from AT&T's dependability.

G1 Cost based price modeling

Another strategy that can be subsumed under the "target pricing" lever is cost based price modeling. Here the aim is to determine the total possible cost of a part on the basis of a cost breakdown, and to then allocate this theoretical cost to the sub-parts. The costs are broken down by processes, i.e. a cost rate is determined for each process step and each unit. Thus, a price for welding is determined depending on the length of the weld. Another example would be hole punching. Cost based price modeling abandons the traditional method of pricing individual parts in favor of pricing individual process steps. The starting point for this method is a cost breakdown by process steps. This can be obtained in any of three ways:

- Have the supplier perform a cost breakdown on the basis of individual process steps. Right from the start, one should ask for offers based on individual process steps rather than individual parts.

- Perform internal comparisons or acquire comparison figures on the basis of internally available cost data for process steps. In this case, the cost breakdown can be performed relatively easily. However, there is the risk of overestimating the costs of individual process steps insofar as internal comparison figures are not comparable with those of external suppliers.

- Perform product-costing analysis. This can be done using internally available information or comparison figures from other suppliers. Once the cost data has been determined, it is ultimately a matter of comparing the most competitive cost items with one other. This can be done either on a best-cost basis or using the top 25 percent (1st quartile principle), so as not to include outliers in the calculation. As a result, the company now has a further basis for determining and asserting target prices.

This form of cost based price modeling is especially suited for B and C parts which, because of the prioritization of A parts, tend to be ignored in traditional tendering processes. With the aid of cost based price modeling, it is also possible to establish and obtain fact-based prices for these parts.

Cost based price modeling is a method that allows the prices of components to be derived using product costs. Thus, the traditional method of comparing prices per part is replaced by a comparison of prices per process step.

> *Case example: Shipyard*
>
> A North German shipyard used the cost breakdown or cost based price modeling method to purchase small welded steel assemblies. In the process of requesting tenders for bigger steel assemblies, the shipyard also asked for a cost breakdown per process step. As usual in such cases, the outcome was unequivocally positive: The bids provided the cost base for individual process steps, which could then be used for product costing analysis with regard to the B and C parts, and hence for determining parts prices. This also made it possible to establish prices for B and C parts for the first time, and thus achieve savings of up to 20 percent. This despite the fact that some observers believe cost breakdowns are generally calculated too optimistically – or one could also say, too realistically.

G2 Cost regression analysis

Cost regression analysis is based on the statistical regression analysis method, which aims to quantify dependencies between different variables and represent them in a mathematical formula. These dependencies can be highly diverse, and can best be illustrated by an example. The price for a hotel room depends on various factors. First, it makes a difference whether the room is in a downtown business hotel, a luxury hotel on the edge of town, or a village guesthouse. It also matters whether the establishment belongs to a chain or is run by a private owner. Other important factors are the size of the hotel, the availability of wellness and fitness facilities, the quality of the restaurant, the scope of special services for regular business customers, and so on. This list is far from complete, but whatever can be qualitatively listed with relative ease can also be represented mathematically with the aid of statistical regression analysis. In the case of hotels, for example, regression analysis allows two general questions to be answered:

- What factors actually influence the room price (and which have no demonstrable influence)?

- What influence does a specific factor actually have on the price?

Cost regression analysis in purchasing looks at such factors as the linear relationship between the costs of an assembly and its technical parameters. Cost regression analysis is thus a form of multi-variant, linear regression analysis. Theoretically, there are no limitations to the application of cost regression analysis. It can be used anytime one wishes to represent dependencies between different variables, as long as the correct explanatory variables are specified. However one should ask at an early stage whether an actual causal connection exists, or whether the correlation being described is merely statistical.

Daily purchasing practice has revealed a number of specific preconditions for the use of cost regression analysis. Only if these are fulfilled can one be fairly certain that the effort and expense involved (e.g. compilation of data) is reasonable and proportionate to the possible benefits of the method. Four criteria are especially important in this context:

- A sufficient level of technical complexity.

- A large number of different variants.

- A large number of components/assemblies.

- Availability of data.

Cost regression analysis is primarily used for commercial applications. It allows one to gain a relatively speedy insight into the price structure of a certain component or assembly at a trans-organizational level. For example, it allows one to determine whether a certain supplier is too expensive with regard to all variants of a component, or only in certain cases. It can also be used to ascertain whether certain business units are consistently purchasing at excessive prices.

This information can be specifically used for renegotiating with suppliers so as to achieve rapid savings: The results of regression analysis allow high-priced parts to be identified in negotiations, which usually leads to price reductions. To conduct these renegotiations successfully, a negotiating strategy must be developed for each supplier, one that considers risk as well as the technology concerned.

With the help of cost regression analysis, one can identify high-price oases for components/assemblies, and reduce (or even eliminate) them quickly through renegotiation. Cost regression analysis can also be used as a partnership tool for determining long-term prices on the basis of technical specifications. The use of regression analysis as a target-price function can also be applied as a tool for structuring consensual, long-term relationships with suppliers. This enables technical optimizations, especially through reductions in variants. Thus, the method impressively and clearly indicates how many variants ("points") of a certain assembly there are in an organization. In practice, this information frequently comes as a surprise, since the actual number of variants tends to be underestimated. Cost regression analysis, with its "clear" representation of variants and costs, allows for a fact-based discussion of variant costs in relation to customer benefits, ultimately reducing the number of variants. The simplification and downgrading of products can also be undertaken with the aid of this strategy. Cost regression analysis not only indicates the number of different variants, but also the number of complexity levels or product groups within one product line. Again, this makes possible a fact-based discussion about the degree to which products can be simplified. Cost regression analysis is therefore recommended not only for reducing costs, but for product development as well.

> *Case example: Transformer purchasing by an energy utility*
>
> The cost drivers identified by an energy utility included not only power performance and charging losses, but also the high dependency on material costs, e.g. for copper. Armed with this knowledge, the utility company was able to conclude new contracts. Kick-back arrangements were concluded, i.e. it was agreed that the buyer should receive a bonus of approximately five percent of annual purchasing volume. Given the near doubling of the copper price and the fact that transformers contain lots of copper, the savings turned out to be huge. Another result was an agreed basis for pricing future orders, seeing as cost drivers will remain the same in the foreseeable future. Last but not least, it was possible to grow many smaller suppliers (e.g. ones that had sold transformers to small businesses) into bigger ones. These were then able to offer prices up to 20 percent below those of previous suppliers, thanks to being aware of the cost drivers on the customer side. By applying this strategy, the utility company was able to identify "high-price oases," which could then be reviewed jointly with the suppliers in renegotiations. It was also able to initiate a sustained technical review, involving purchasing, engineering, as well as its suppliers.

G3 Price benchmark

Price benchmarking is a flexible and comparatively simple method of analyzing the price situation for different components or material groups. It involves comparing the prices of a company's sourcing category with the prices paid by other companies under similar conditions and with the same specifications. As with every comparison, the improvement potential is indicated by the difference between the two figures.

Price benchmarking is only possible for identical or similar products. If differences are found, the values have to be "normalized." The price benchmark can be applied not only to unit prices or price distributions, but also to contract conditions. Unit price benchmark consists quite simply of comparing unit prices. To take account of price discounts or other allowances (as customary with software), unit price benchmarks are often also compared on the basis of price corridors. Price distribution benchmarking is especially suited for services of all kinds, e.g. IT services.

To perform the comparison, distinctions are made between different levels of skills or services. A project manager, for instance, must have different abilities than a technical assistant or a consultant. Benchmarking of contract terms is done by comparing the individual parts of agreements. The aim is to analyze contracts with regard to pricing options and search for references to possible price adjustments. To this end, comparisons can be based on external price indices or information provided by suppliers with regard to their cost structure. New contracts can then be negotiated using the resulting data and benchmarks.

Case example: Price benchmark in the context of M&A in the packing industry

A leading producer of flexible packing acquired a competing company with the same product portfolio. The companies wanted to prepare for integration and take measures to achieve purchasing synergies even before the antitrust reviews were completed. In this phase, however, the companies were not allowed and/or did not wish to compare their prices, with the result that A.T. Kearney was called in to set up a "clean room." This involved comparing the material prices of similar parts from the same suppliers in order to identify synergies. These synergies were then compared in an aggregated, anonymous way. Comparison between the terms of the two companies was further supplemented by external benchmarks. Thanks to this preparation, it was possible to achieve cost savings of between 15 and 30 percent in the first quarter after completion of the acquisition.

Total cost of ownership

Although total cost of ownership (TCO) has been part of the purchaser's toolbox for years, it is understood and applied to varying degrees. TCO encompasses all the costs arising from the purchase, utilization, maintenance and ultimate disposal of a product within a company. Anyone who investigates all the influencing factors will acquire insights that facilitate comparison between two suppliers. Hidden costs, which often far exceed primary costs, will be rendered visible. Only with this big picture in mind one can meaningfully compare suppliers with one another and develop effective sourcing strategies.

In the best case, the TCO strategy can lead to value creation partnerships whose focus is not exclusively on price reductions. TCO also helps to eliminate activities that do not contribute value from the lifecycle of a product or service. Moreover, the savings possible through strategic purchasing can be more accurately predicted by TCO than by other means. The process is simple and follows logical rules.

The first step is to define all relevant costs (particularly material costs, production costs, etc.), followed by cost drivers, and to then calculate the costs for each part. This is facilitated by integrating the TCO strategy at an early stage of a tendering process. Thus, basic costs of the company can be completely depicted, allowing RFPs to be compared.

All in all, a disciplined and structured approach is critical in focusing on those cost components that can be most easily influenced. The application of TCO is particularly worthwhile in certain areas:

- Transport: What is the cheapest method for shipping materials, and how does this differ from the current method? Can packaging material be returned, for example?

- Parts logistics: How can parts logistics in the production process be improved? How can the throughput time of parts deliveries be shortened? How can inventory costs be reduced?

- Set-up times: What causes the longest set-up times? Are there other machines that could be used in order to shorten set-up times?

- Production process: How should volumes be changed so as to justify either a manual or an automated process? What would be the most difficult, most expensive, most time-consuming component?

- Administration/indirect costs: Is there a more efficient interface with ordering systems? What could be achieved by changing the duration of contracts?

It will be clear by now that TCO should be part of any sourcing process. Only then can total costs be meaningfully included in all deliberations. This especially applies to the procurement of sophisticated capital goods, to the pooling of purchasing for the whole company, and the consolidation of redundant parts numbers.

A total cost overview can also produce many positive effects in other areas: Contract damages can be avoided, simulations can be used in advance of prototyping, and returnable packing materials can be employed, etc. Other possibilities are the use of EDI or a simple evaluation of the profitability of individual suppliers.

Case example: Total costs at a rolling mill

In virtually no other area is TCO orientation so deeply rooted as in the rolling mills of the steel industry. Rollers are of key importance in transforming ingots into products sold to end customers, i.e. in the form of sheet steel, section steel or pipes. Some rollers embody so much know-how that they are protected by patents. At the same time, rollers are wearing parts that have to be periodically replaced. Premature roller replacement caused by breakage means a disruption to production that is both unwelcome and costly. In the industry, the costs of rollers are stated not in US dollars per machine, but in US dollars per ton of steel rolled. This cost therefore covers not just the purchase price for the rollers, but the total costs incurred in rolling one ton. When purchasing rollers, total costs per ton are also the benchmark for choosing a supplier.

G5 Supplier development

Even after a painstaking selection process, a company rarely finds the perfect supplier right off the bat. Only a process of supplier development, which can take several months or even years, will turn the supplier into the reliable partner the company needs.

Supplier development can be used with both new and existing suppliers. As a rule, however, "new" is the key characteristic for supplier development. This can mean that a certain product line/portfolio has not been covered by the supplier so far, or that a previously unimportant supplier is to be developed into a key one. Or it may mean finding a completely new supplier for the company, with the supplier perhaps still in the process of being set up. Whatever the case, the focus is on the relationship with the supplier, and for this reason the term used in the literature is "supplier development." Only where there is high demand power can new suppliers be built up. The process of developing and implementing meaningful strategies can be divided into four steps:

- Taking stock: The current relationships and development potential with regard to an appropriate number of suppliers (20 to 30) must be identified, and the results recorded in an aggregate summary for an overview of the supplier situation.

- Creation of appropriate supplier strategies: Assessment criteria for suppliers are drawn up and agreed upon with all stakeholders in joint workshops.

- Development of tools for strategy implementation: The focus is on developing an implementation plan with the appropriate tools. These include instruments such as a scorecard covering all key parameters, e.g. from purchasing volume to supplier dependability, competitiveness, etc.

- Implementation of measures and reporting on the results.

Best practice strategies for recruiting and developing suppliers show how successful companies develop their suppliers. Resources must be made available and dedicated to the development of suppliers and joint offerings, thus creating a relationship that generates more value than before. The important thing is to focus not just on the home region, but to think globally and develop globally. To ensure that this happens, suppliers must be involved in the customer's business processes, pledged to the same goals and, if possible, certified. Communication must be open and leave room for learning on both sides.

It should be apparent that some of these best practice strategies also lead to nearby fields of the chessboard. In any case, the key to supplier development is purposefully enhancing the supplier relationship and growing the supplier into an enterprise that is able to make an important contribution with regard to purchased parts.

Besides the development of new suppliers, the process may also involve cultivating existing suppliers and developing them further for the supply of new products.

Another case in which supplier development may be applied is that of a particularly low-price supplier who does not (yet) meet the purchasing company's requirements, either in technical or quality terms.

Any company that decides to undertake supplier development has to be prepared "to put its money where its mouth is," but will harvest positive returns eventually. The company's financial commitment can take various forms: investment, volume guarantees, exchange of know-how, initial price premiums, etc. Provided the collaboration is of a long-term nature, any amount can be considered well spent.

Case example: Development of a supplier for the food industry

Peppermint tea tastes good and is in ever increasing demand, as the sales figures of tea producers attest. Like good wine, good peppermint does not grow everywhere; there are only a few regions in the world where peppermint can be found in the desired quality. One of these is Bulgaria.

While there are a few industrially run companies that manage peppermint cultures, most of the tea industry's suppliers are small firms that almost resemble mom-and-pop growing operations. These produce top quality peppermint and have the necessary growing expertise. However, they lack the financial resources to build their farms into small industrial enterprises and thus increase output to the levels demanded by tea producers.

A tea producer's relationship with an ambitious supplier had gone well, with no quality complaints for a period of some five years; however, the capacity limits of this peppermint producer were eventually reached. The producer therefore decided to embark on a supplier development program. This encompassed investments by the tea producer (land and machinery), purchase guarantees for coming years, and support from the tea producer in establishing quality processes.

What the tea producer received in return was a price guarantee for the following three years (despite rising raw material prices), an increase in supply security, and repayment on current account for its investment through quantities supplied – a classic win-win situation!

G6 Total lifecycle concept

All products – whether cars, fast-moving consumer goods or high-value capital goods – have their own individual lifecycles. When falling sales indicate that a product lifecycle is nearing its end, the company has to go back to the drawing board, either modifying the product to bring it back into line with customer requirements, or putting a completely new product on the market.

The total lifecycle concept attempts to describe the collaboration with suppliers from the product's market launch right through to the end of its presence on the market. Each product passes through five typical lifecycle phases. Before the product is launched, it has to be developed and its marketability tested. This is followed by five stages, each one of different length:

- Introduction phase: During the introduction phase, sales rise slowly, depending on the marketing push. However, no profit is earned at this stage due to previously incurred product development costs and ongoing spending on communication. The introduction phase already decides whether and how well the product is accepted by the market. This phase ends when break-even is reached.

- Growth phase: During this phase, profits are made for the first time. It is characterized by rapid growth, accelerated by further intense marketing activity, and ends as soon as the sales curve becomes digressive.

- Maturity phase: As the product no longer requires intense advertising and economies of scale are able to take effect, the highest profits can now be recorded. Later in this phase, however, profits decline because of increasing competition. Nevertheless, this is when the product has the highest market share.

- Saturation phase: As soon as there is no more market growth ahead, the saturation phase begins. Now, both sales revenue and profits decline. This phase can be extended through modifications and product re-launching.

- Degeneration phase: Finally, the market shrinks. It is no longer possible to stem the fall in sales revenue, and market share is inevitably lost. Profits also fall, and the time has come to readjust the product portfolio.

To earn high sales revenue and profits for as long as possible with one product generation, one must enhance the product's attractiveness from time to time. In the auto industry, the terms "major product upgrade" or a "facelift" are used. In both cases, the basic technical structure of the product remains largely unchanged. Usually only those components subject to short innovation cycles (e.g. electronics) or fashion trends are replaced.

To ensure that product upgrades/facelifts can be carried out on reasonable economic terms, the milestones of the product lifecycle are defined in advance with suppliers. The total lifecycle concept then determines in detail how sales revenue, and in particular the costs for upgrades/facelifts, are shared between the company and suppliers over the complete product lifecycle.

Case example: Product lifecycles in the military equipment field

Apart from the auto industry, good examples of total lifecycle concepts can also be found in the field of military equipment. To keep their budgets under control, militaries regularly update their existing systems rather than procure new ones. A record-holder in this regard is the Boeing B-52. Developed in the late 1940s as a high-altitude nuclear bomber, its maiden flight took place on April 15, 1952. Of the 744 aircraft made, over 90 are still in service. It is currently intended that the bomber will remain in service till around 2040, making it the military aircraft with the longest service life in history. It is already the case today that most B-52 pilots are younger than the aircraft they are flying!

Over the years, the B-52 has undergone repeated modernization. Thus, from 1971 to 1976, all the 270 B-52G and B-52H planes still in operation were equipped with an electro-optical system for low-level missions, consisting of an infrared camera and a lens with residual light amplifier. This was followed in the 1980s by further modernization and new weapons. An avionics program was implemented from 1980 to 1986. From 1982 to 2005, the B-52s were the only aircraft of the US armed forces to be upgraded with cruise missiles. 1994 saw a further electronics upgrade with GPS receivers and encoded communications. On June 16, 2006, the Pentagon announced that Boeing had been awarded a contract worth 150 million US dollars for a program known as "Smart Weapons Integration Next Generation" (SWING), to modernize the weapons electronics and mounting systems on the B-52s by the end of 2020.

Project based partnership

Project based partnerships represent a meaningful form of cooperation between two or more companies wishing to collaborate for only a defined period of time or within a defined scope of activity. Project based partnerships are especially suitable if the intention is to utilize each other's capabilities without being committed to a long-term partnership. This can make sense, for example, when a purchasing company is looking for a development supplier to develop a new product. In this case, the project based partnership is limited to the lifetime of the product and to the scope of the defined product. Project based partnerships are intended to produce results relatively quickly; to ensure their success, four preconditions must be in place. First, the distribution of tasks and competencies between the two partners must be clearly defined. This avoids demarcation disputes and duplication of activities. Second, a clear timetable must be drawn up for the joint project, with clear deadlines and milestones. The timetable ensures that the project is implemented in a purposeful manner. It should also incorporate the following: adequate buffer times to allow for unforeseen events; possible correction scenarios; various exit scenarios in case certain milestones should not be met; a winding-up program for the end of the project. The third important factor for a project based partnership is a clearly defined steering organization. A mechanism must be put in place for taking the final decisions and for mediation in the event of disputes. The final important factor is a clear definition of how the fruits of the project are to be shared between the partners.

Besides these systematic aspects, a project based partnership also requires a high level of trust and cooperation between the two partners (despite being limited in time and scope).

> *Case example: Development of the exhaust system for a high-performance car*
>
> A supplier of exhaust systems is selected by an automaker for a project to develop a new high-performance car. The supplier is commissioned to supply the complete exhaust system, consisting of manifold, catalytic converter, front pipe, front muffler, intermediate pipe, intermediate muffler, rear muffler, exhaust flap and tail pipe. The sound of the exhaust, developed with the aid of sound engineering, is a trademark characteristic of the automobile brand. Thus, engineers from the two companies work in close collaboration right from the start of the project. Resident engineers of the supplier are present on-site at the automaker until the launch of series production, and contribute their special skills whenever needed. After the successful rollout of series production, the supplier's development team moves on to the next project, either at the same automaker or at one of its competitors.

G8 Profit sharing

Profit sharing means completely involving the supplier in a company's business opportunities and risks. A precondition is that the supplier must exercise an outstanding influence on the success of the business. As the term "profit" leaves much room for interpretation, clear rules and mutual trust between the customer and the supplier are essential.

As the business is dependent on the participation of both partners, both also strive for profit sharing.

Case example: Prospecting and exploration

While the production of mineral resources is in the hands of global giants with deep pockets, the process of prospecting and exploring is mostly done by small firms. There are several thousand such small exploration companies throughout the world looking for new deposits of gold, silver, copper, zinc, platinum, uranium and other metals and minerals. If successful, these small firms then sell their mining rights to major companies.

According to the *Handelsblatt* newspaper (March 3, 2008) – a leading European newspaper – 11.4 billion US dollars were invested in prospecting and exploration in 2007 alone – an increase of 40 percent over the previous year. It should be noted, however, that exploration costs (personnel, fuel, and equipment) have also risen sharply.

Many new exploration companies are established by expert geologists who form hypotheses about the location of deposits from their scientific work. In the absence of a track record, however, it is virtually impossible for them to obtain funding from the stock market or banks. Still, they need suitable equipment to verify their theories. In such cases, specialist equipment suppliers will assume the risk and offer the exploration start-up firm the necessary equipment in return for a share in the profits. If the firm's hypothesis was wrong and the anticipated deposits are not found, the equipment supplier is left empty-handed. On the other hand, if the exploration firm was right and exploitation rights are sold to one of the big mining companies, the equipment supplier will be entitled to a hefty share of the return.

H1 Linear performance pricing

Most companies lack a sound, objective basis for defining target prices. The linear performance pricing strategy is one way to identify a technical cost driver that is crucial for the product price of a sourcing category, which can then serve as the basis of objective target prices.

In the case of simple components where the crucial cost driver is evident (e.g. weight) a straightforward "rule-of-three" calculation is sufficient to determine the target price. Simple steel parts, products sold by the yard/meter, etc. are good examples.

The method may appear straightforward at first sight; however, the devil is in the details. The crucial cost driver is not always so easy to identify. Then there are cases in which the cost effect is far from clear. In the case of a casting, for example, both the weight and also the cross-section area of the mold can be relevant cost drivers.

The challenge is to pick the crucial cost driver out of all the possible ones. An appropriate method for this is simple correlation analysis. The result indicates the strength of the correlation between the cost driver and the price. The cost driver with the highest correlation to the price is the relevant one. After identifying the relevant cost driver with the aid of correlation analysis, the target price can then be determined, again using a rule-of-three calculation.

To be able to use linear performance pricing, however, the following preconditions must be met. There must be only one relevant cost driver, which usually means that the item concerned must be relatively simple. Simple parts that contain a large proportion of raw material are highly suited to this method, e.g. simple castings, crude steel, copper wire, etc. More complex parts, e.g. those involving various process steps, are not suited for linear performance pricing.

> *Case example: Non-machined parts procurement by an automotive supplier*
>
> A company working in the automotive supply industry buys non-machined sand castings. The weight of a casting is used as a point of departure for reviewing the plausibility of the supplier's prices. After detailed analysis of other conceivable cost drivers, it emerges that the cross-sectional area of the mold has a statistically higher correlation to the price of the component. With this knowledge, more accurate target prices can be specified in future, and costly inexactitudes avoided. Adopting the cross-sectional area as the basis of calculation allows the company to identify potential savings averaging 14 percent (up to 40 percent in individual cases).

H2 Factor cost analysis

Who has not read about the low cost of labor in China or India? The costs for the resource "labor" obviously differ enormously across the world; in extreme cases, labor costs amount to only 1/50 of those in the US. But also the costs of land, rent, waste disposal or energy can differ widely in price.

The aim of factor cost analysis is to render these differences visible and allow them to be exploited. It involves identifying the resources required by the existing supplier to make a product. This information is supplemented by cost-driver data, e.g. set-up times, productivity, machine-hour rates, or alternative prices for principal materials. After making the above transparent, one compares the data with that of other suppliers or other regions, in order to develop strategies for optimizing the cost structure in a targeted fashion. The aim is to create a basis for choosing measures to be implemented by the supplier. Thus measures for cutting the costs of materials may include providing one's own sub-suppliers, or (if the share of staff costs is high) even suggesting the possibility of relocation.

> *Case example: Harnesses at a maker of railway rolling stock*
>
> A maker of railway rolling stock wished to reduce the cost of purchasing large, heavy and inadequately specified harnesses, and therefore applied the strategy of factor cost analysis. The analysis indicated that, due to the high share of personnel costs, production in the nearby Czech Republic would be cheaper. The existence of local materials suppliers also meant that material-related savings were possible for the harnesses. On this basis, the supplier was advised to open a new plant in the Czech Republic in order to achieve sustained reductions in the cost of harnesses. Implementation of this strategy led to a cut in supplier's costs of around 30 percent.

H3 Unbundled prices

In the past, there was a trend for companies to purchase modules or systems, specifically as a way of reducing the complexity of their own purchasing. This frequently resulted in loss of technological or commercial transparency, particularly for parts with a high share of service or development costs, or those bought as a complete system but having clearly definable components.

Unbundling of prices addresses this challenge and generates transparency with regard to the price structure of a module or system. It does so by breaking down the total price of a product or service into the relevant price elements for individual components or process steps. The price transparency gained in this way can then be used for determining target prices.

After breaking down modules or systems into smaller components or process steps, target costs for the individual part-products can be identified in one of two ways: either by submitting an inquiry to potential suppliers for the individual component, or by determining target costs using cost analyses based on specific cost drivers (e.g. cost regression analysis, cost-based price modeling, etc.).

The resulting price transparency for individual components can be exploited in different ways. First, it can be used in re-negotiations with the system supplier. Second, the buying company may stipulate the use of parts by lower-cost suppliers. Third, it may be able to abandon system purchasing altogether and buy components instead.

> *Case example: Purchase of synchronization by a gearbox producer*
>
> A producer of gearboxes purchased the synchronization from a 2nd tier supplier in the form of a complete system. Apart from moderate annual price cuts, virtually no savings were achieved in recent years. Moreover, it was difficult to change suppliers for the complete system: For one thing, the number of suppliers was limited; for another, the synchronization had been designed with this 2nd tier supplier in mind.

> Thus, the gearbox producer suspected that there was a lot of untapped savings potential with regard to the synchronization. Since the strategy of putting the complete system out to tender did not appear very promising, the gearbox producer performed analyses to identify the prices for individual components of the synchronization (e.g. cone ring, synchronizer ring, synchronizer hub, clutch body). In addition, the producer asked for prices from other component suppliers. The producer then used this unbundling of the synchronization price to demand price cuts from the existing system supplier. It also linked these demands for price cuts to the need to utilize components supplied by manufacturers in low-cost countries. Altogether, the gearbox producer succeeded in reducing the total cost of the synchronization by a two-digit percentage.

H4 Leverage market imbalances

Market imbalances are a phenomenon that usually only exists in economic theory. In this strategy, the aim is to systematically identify market imbalances and exploit them for purchasing purposes. Such imbalances can come about as a result of differing capacity utilization across certain regions, variable price mechanisms, or currency fluctuations.

Market imbalances can be recognized by checking core indicators for certain supplier markets at regular intervals. These core indicators include national price indices for various material groups (in combination with exchange rates), or capacity utilization figures for certain industries. By examining differences in these core indices or by making comparisons across countries, one can get a good overview of the materials costs. It may be found, for instance, that certain cost developments are restricted to a specific region and can be circumvented by changing to a supplier in another country.

> *Case example: Purchasing of welded steel components by a maker of tramcars*
>
> Until recently, a maker of tramcars was purchasing welded steel parts from Western European suppliers. However, heavy market demand and the resulting high level of capacity utilization at existing suppliers drove up prices by some 20 percent. Unfortunately, the tramcar maker was not in a position to switch suppliers at short notice. Basically, the supplier had the tramcar maker "over a barrel." The tramcar maker found a solution after a pragmatic review of capacity utilization in other industries across various countries. It was found, for instance, that Eastern European shipyards had come under pressure from Asian competitors and were suffering from severe overcapacity. The tramcar maker was therefore able to obtain attractive competing offers from qualified suppliers. While a change of supplier was not possible on short notice, a credible announcement that other suppliers were available was enough to ward off the threatened price increases. The tramcar maker made use of the following years to build relationships with these new suppliers, testing and approving their products.

H5 Supplier fitness program

Fitness is just as important for a supplier partnering up with a customer as it is for an employee hiring himself out to an employer. In sports, fitness programs have the goal of burning excess fat, building muscle fiber, and achieving a sound and balanced physique. Many people engage a personal trainer to design a fitness program matched to their individual needs and using the right approach.

The same is also true of a supplier fitness program which, by finding the right strategies and employing the right levers, helps a company's supplier eliminate weaknesses and become more competitive, i.e. by identifying and implementing cost reduction potential.

In contrast to supplier development, which primarily strives to create new suppliers or increase the use of existing smaller suppliers, supplier fitness programs focus on existing large suppliers. The object is to improve the supplier's cost position. This encompasses numerous measures that have a direct or indirect impact on costs and that are developed and implemented through a structured program:

- Preparation and selection phase: Supplier fitness programs are a complicated matter and cannot be undertaken for all suppliers. (Consider how complex this would be if an industrial company has some 8,000 group suppliers, for example.) Thus, one must select appropriate suppliers to include in the program. This in turn requires the creation of sector-specific questionnaires, as well as the internal and external analysis of product/process benchmark data. At the same time, visits to the supplier have to be planned. The aim of this preliminary work is to gain an understanding of the entire cost structure and product portfolio of the supplier.

- Opportunity scan phase: Evaluation of the supplier initially means analyzing its processes, with a particular focus on purchasing and production. After identifying the cost-cutting levers, concrete activities that can boost the supplier's fitness are devised, reviewed and recorded. Each of these levers must be based on positively identified cost improvement potential.

- Implementation phase: The measures are implemented in close collaboration between the supplier and the customer, initially in a pilot area. The pilot project is then successively extended throughout the supplier's operation.

- Reporting phase: Implementation results and the consistency of implementation are kept under constant review.

As many companies are not able to maintain the broad base of in-house expertise required for this activity, consultants are frequently called in at this stage to work on supplier fitness in joint client/consultant teams.

Case example: Injection-control system at a producer of consumer electronics

A producer of high-quality consumer electronics found itself caught in the margin trap. On the one side, the market expected constantly falling prices paired with ever better performance. On the other hand, suppliers were increasing their prices due to rising raw material costs. This situation became particularly pressing with regard to housing components made of injection-molded plastic.

The supplier of the housings justified its prices based not only on raw material costs, but also on extremely tight production tolerances. The latter entailed an unusually high volume of rejects, which had to be sorted out by hand by the supplier. In the course of a supplier fitness program, particular attention was paid to this aspect. It soon became clear that the control setting for the injection nozzle, which was primarily based on empirical values, was causing the high level of rejects.

The supplier was advised to install a special instrumentation and control system which would automatically adjust the nozzle on the strength of feedback from heat sensors in the cavity of the injection mold. Thanks to this moderate investment, the rate of rejects fell to almost zero, while the consumer electronics producer paid twelve percent less for parts. In addition, the producer of injection moldings could now exploit the instrumentation and control system for all its customers, to the benefit of its own competitiveness and bottom line.

H6 Collaborative cost reduction

Companies often have only a small development department, but a large number of suppliers. Collaborative cost reduction enables the experience and intellectual capital of suppliers to be used to supplement a company's own development capabilities. The suppliers are closely involved in the process of making cost cuts, and in return, the savings are shared. Sharing in the savings gives the suppliers a strong incentive to help find new cost-cutting ideas, and to communicate these to the customer.

To achieve a spirit of partnership and open cooperation between equals, it is essential to initiate a process of systematic communication with those suppliers who have been identified as the best candidates. It is especially helpful to communicate the intention to share savings in a clear and forthright way.

As a first step, all the ideas contributed by the suppliers are collected. A useful aid in this process can be sending out a standardized form to suppliers. Where a large number of suppliers and lots of individual contributors are involved, this can be facilitated by making the form accessible online. Besides a description of the idea, other important information on the form includes the amount of potential savings, the possible timing of implementation, the likelihood of implementation and the effort/expense involved. This basic information will facilitate rapid prioritization and selection of ideas.

Selected ideas offered by suppliers are then reviewed in terms of feasibility in a discussion process that includes the engineering, quality, production and controlling departments, etc. Naturally, it is often the case that the supplier has failed to consider the bigger picture or certain knock-on effects, and that the idea is therefore not feasible. But if there is nothing standing in the way, a business case and an implementation plan can be drawn up, and the appropriate responsibilities defined.

Special importance should be attached to subsequent controlling of implementation. Many companies develop lots of ideas with their suppliers, but as no one feels genuinely responsible for them, they are allowed to fail in implementation.

One of the most important factors for success is ruthless prioritization and selection of the ideas. During the creative brainstorming process, it is perfectly legitimate to consider any and all concepts. Subsequently, however, a rapid selection must be made, or too many flimsy ideas will tie up resources needed elsewhere and get in the way of implementation. In this context, the warning about "not being able to see the forest for the trees" is very apt.

> *Case example: Collaborative cost reduction at a maker of household appliances*
>
> A maker of household appliances had achieved various cost cuts by putting items out to tender and conducting annual price negotiations. To identify further potential, a collaborative cost reduction program was initiated. The aim of the program was to generate, assess and implement ideas for sustained cost cutting in collaboration with the biggest suppliers. The whole initiative was supported by broad-based communication on the top-management level. This included a personal letter of invitation from the purchasing director to the management officers of the top suppliers, a video message via the internet, and the holding of a special supplier day.

> As a consequence, over 1,000 ideas were submitted within four weeks by the top 50 suppliers, and were documented, assessed and implemented by the maker of household appliances. The cost-cutting ideas, which covered the complete process chain, included bundling call-forward order volumes, replacing disposable packing with returnable packing, and measures for making quality requirements less stringent.

H7 Value based sourcing

Besides helping cut material costs, suppliers can also contribute significantly to increasing value through innovation. Suppliers not only have the ability to offer favorably priced products, but considerable knowledge as well – e.g. on the competitive environment, the market, technologies, and even the internal processes and specific challenges of their customers. Properly used, this knowledge represents the most important part of the value contributed by a given supplier. A supplier can generate value for its customers in many different ways, e.g. through a reduction in time to market, better product quality, or strengthened brand awareness.

But systematic use of a supplier's know-how is often just the beginning.

Value based sourcing is a strategy whereby suppliers are selected in terms of their capabilities and are continually encouraged to innovate, the goal being value maximization.

Roughly speaking, the value based sourcing method consists of a "value definition" and a "value generation" phase and has two goals: First, selecting value drivers and appropriate suppliers; second, fostering the sustainable exchange of know-how with these suppliers.

In implementing the value based sourcing process, seven primary factors are crucial for success:

- Focus: Supplier selection and the exchange of know-how must be focused in order to prevent a flood of ideas, a large proportion of which may turn out to be useless.

- Governance: Targeted value generation requires an interdisciplinary team, with clear decision-making and escalation mechanisms.

- Discipline: The team members must assume responsibility for the collaboration, as well as for documenting tasks and responsibilities.

- Trust: Suppliers must be secure in the knowledge that their ideas will not be made accessible to other suppliers. Tangible confidence-building measures are therefore part of the process.

- Incentives: The suppliers must be offered the right structural and/or financial incentives, e.g. in the form of profit sharing.

- Process interface: Value generation requires active interfacing with numerous processes within the company, e.g. innovation or product planning.

- Tools and systems: Web-based instruments for the evaluation and follow-up of supplier ideas, along with a well-functioning collaboration platform, support the process of identifying ideas.

Value based sourcing requires a mandate for purchasing that exceeds the powers normally granted to it. The increased use of supplier capabilities in generating value raises the strategic importance of purchasing within an organization.

> *Case example: Headlamps that support brand identity*
>
> The automotive supplier Hella and BMW joined forces to give the BMW 5 Series, which was due for a facelift, a truly new look. Hella offered circular light conductors to underscore BMW's twin headlamps. Hella's idea was well received – it meant that BMWs were the only cars immediately recognizable in the dark. In order to fully exploit this boost to the brand image, the technology was used on almost a complete generation of BMW models.

H8 Strategic alliance

Strategic alliances especially make sense when two companies have complementary capabilities and each contributes equally to the partnership. Strategic alliances with suppliers, i.e. long-term collaboration with a particular partner, often come about when one of the companies is unwilling or unable to maintain certain strategic capabilities in-house, or has no possibility to integrate vertically.

A strategic alliance between companies can be used, for instance, as a means of avoiding supply bottlenecks in times of high capacity utilization.

The core aspect of a strategic alliance is that it is designed for the long term, i.e. is not subject to any project-oriented limits. This of course does not mean that strategic alliances are intended to last forever, since they may become obsolete in the event of a change in strategic direction by one of the companies. Nonetheless, a characteristic feature of a strategic alliance is the long-term intention of the partnership.

In forming a strategic alliance, attention has to be paid to certain matters. First, a management model has to be defined. Management models may take the form of ordinary business agreements, e.g. simple outsourcing contracts. Besides the management model, however, the issue of mutual control also needs to be defined. A strategic alliance must be based on mutual trust and openness.

Strategic alliances also call for effective risk management. The more unstable, unpredictable, change-oriented and dynamic a market is, the greater is the risk associated with relying on just one partner. The purchasing company must therefore be sufficiently flexible to correct the course of the alliance, or even end it, in a timely manner.

The selection and assessment of the partners is the basis for building a strategic alliance. Alongside the assessment phase, the selection process should also allow sufficient room for negotiations, giving both sides the opportunity to introduce themselves and to question the concepts of the other side. Only then need the formal aspects be discussed and agreed in writing. Once the alliance is established, managing the relationship (which will not be the only close cooperation in purchasing) will be a highly demanding process.

Without a governance model that includes the factors crucial for success or failure, it will be difficult to maintain the relationship over time. Where a partnership already exists, there are various possibilities for making it more stable and productive. In this context, various questions pose themselves: Does my partner fulfill the requirements that help me keep my value promise? What capabilities of the partner can I use as assets on the market? Could other partners contribute just as much? On the other hand, how important and how effective is our own performance for our partner(s)? Could our contribution to the alliance also be provided by other companies?

Is the relationship built on give and take, or does one side contribute more than the other?

In general, all companies seeking new alliances, or wishing to maintain existing ones in the long term, should communicate openly and directly with each other, especially in the event of problems. And in case the ownership of a partner should change, it is advisable, despite all the integration, to maintain market transparency in such a way that outsiders can still clearly see which partner makes which contribution.

Case example: "SMART alliance"

SMART is the company in the automobile sector with the shallowest manufacturing depth, with no less than 90 percent of added value contributed by suppliers. To perfect the cooperation, SMART has entered into a strategic alliance with five system partners, known collectively as the "SMART alliance". ThyssenKrupp supplies the rear-axle drive, Magna International makes the SMART's passenger safety cell, the paintwork is done by Paintshop SMART, Continental is responsible for the cockpit module, Plastal produces the body panels, and Magna Uniport contributes the doors and hatch modules. This shallow manufacturing depth is also reflected in the number of employees: While SMART itself has a workforce of around 1,000, the personnel at the "SMART alliance" partners are about double that number. SMART's production completely dispenses with inventories; all parts are delivered just-in-time and just-in-sequence. This means that all suppliers have access to the individual order data for a vehicle, and that they deliver the parts in exactly the sequence required by the SMART plant. SMART's main responsibility is the final, overall testing.

5 Closing Remarks

With its 64 fields and 64 individual methods applicable to all industries, the Purchasing Chessboard™ represents the complete know-how of A.T. Kearney, the leading management consulting company in the field of procurement. This valuable tool clearly demonstrates that there is no sourcing situation in business that cannot be managed using a tried-and-tested, universally adaptable strategy. Thus, the Purchasing Chessboard™ provides a reliable holistic framework for purchasing activities – even on a seller's market.

But the Purchasing Chessboard™ has other uses as well, e.g. for visualizing the skills development of purchasing personnel. The strategies that a member of the purchasing staff has already mastered can be ticked off, while the others can be discussed as part of further development under a goal-setting agreement for the years to come. Once an employee is able to apply all 64 fields of the Purchasing Chessboard™, he/she will have earned the right to be called an "all-rounder." The ultimate goal of the Purchasing Chessboard™ is to trigger a skills-improvement campaign in purchasing, and to help make purchasing a genuinely attractive career stage within a company.

Knowledge is the only tool that does not wear out through frequent use, but actually gets sharper over time. Thus, we as the authors of this book are very much interested in having readers share their experiences in using the Purchasing Chessboard™. A dedicated website has been created to provide a platform for this exchange of views between the authors and readers, and also among readers themselves:

www.purchasingchessboard.com

The website will be used to report continuously on new developments associated with the Purchasing Chessboard™. We hope you have enjoyed this book and that it will contribute to your success!

Appendix

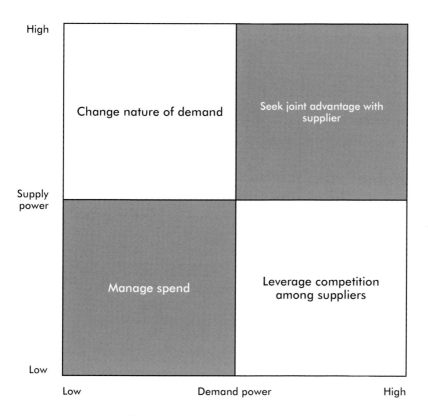

Fig. 8. 4 Purchasing strategies

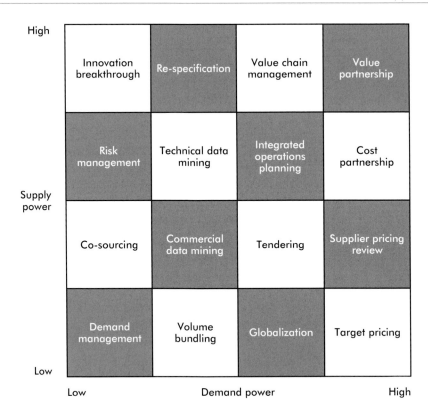

Fig. 9. 16 levers

About the authors

Christian Schuh is co-leader of A.T. Kearney's Operations Practice in Central Europe and is based in Vienna, Austria. He joined A.T. Kearney 15 years ago and has since then led multiple projects for clients in the automotive, construction equipment, defense, packaging, and steel industry in Austria, France, Germany, the UK, Ukraine and the USA. His areas of expertise include strategic sourcing, product development and organization. He is the author of various books, monographs and articles. Before he joined A.T. Kearney he had worked several years for Unilever. Christian Schuh studied aeronautical engineering at TU Graz (Austria) and holds a doctorate degree in business administration. He currently lives in Vienna.

Robert Kromoser has been with A.T. Kearney for 10 years. He currently lives in Austria, however gained most of his consulting experience abroad in Germany, France, Italy, Great Britain and the USA. He is a member of the Operations Practice with a focus on strategic sourcing and cost reduction. He has led multiple projects in the automotive, construction equipment, mechanical engineering, and steel industry. In several studies, he analyzed the role of strategic sourcing as a value-adding factor. Robert Kromoser studied business administration at Vienna University of Economics and Business Administration (Austria) and Carnegie Mellon University (USA).

About the authors

Michael F. Strohmer is a member of the Operations Practice from A.T. Kearney's Vienna office, Austria. In his eight years with the firm, he has led projects at a broad range of international clients, mainly in post merger situations. His work encompassed the mechanical engineering and plant construction, automotive, defense, food & beverage, packaging, and steel sectors. He is an expert on supply management, post merger management and large-scale CAPEX projects. He has published several books and articles on post merger management and is a frequent speaker on these topics at international conferences. Michael F. Strohmer holds a doctorate degree in business administration and law from Johannes-Kepler-University Linz (Austria), where his work focused on Merger Management. He currently lives in Altmünster at lake Traun.

Ramón Romero Pérez joined A.T. Kearney in Berlin, Germany five years ago and is a member of the Operations Practice. He has conducted and led multiple projects for clients in the mechanical engineering, automotive, construction equipment, utility, and steel industry. He is an expert in supply management and asset investment strategies. He is active in academic research on post-merger integration and its impact on purchasing. He is a trainer in negotiation strategies and application of advanced sourcing methodologies. In addition, he has published multiple articles on these topics. Ramón Romero Pérez studied business administration at WHU Vallendar (Germany), Kobe University (Japan) and Manchester Business School (UK). He currently lives in Hamburg (Germany).

The Purchasing Chessboard ™

A.T. KEARNEY

Supply power	A (Low)	B	C	D	E	F	G	H (High)
8 (High)	Invention on demand	Leverage innovation network	Functionality assessment	Specification assessment	Value chain reconfiguration	Revenue sharing	Profit sharing	Strategic alliance
7	Core cost analysis	Design for sourcing	Product teardown	Design for manufacture	Supplier tiering	Sustainability management	Project based partnership	Value based sourcing
6	Vertical integration	Intelligent deal structure	Composite benchmark	Process benchmark	Collaborative capacity management	Virtual inventory management	Total life cycle concept	Collaborative cost reduction
5	Bottleneck management	Political framework management	Product benchmark	Complexity reduction	Visible process organization	Vendor managed inventory	Supplier development	Supplier fitness program
4	Sourcing community	Buying consortia	Cost data mining	Standardization	RFI/RFP process	Expressive bidding	Total cost of ownership	Leverage market imbalances
3	Procurement outsourcing	Mega supplier strategy	Master data management	Spend transparency	Supplier market intelligence	Reverse auctions	Price benchmark	Unbundled prices
2	Compliance management	Closed loop spend management	Supplier consolidation	Bundling across generations	Make or buy	Best shoring	Cost regression analysis	Factor cost analysis
1 (Low)	Demand reduction	Contract management	Bundling across product lines	Bundling across sites	Global sourcing	LCC sourcing	Cost based price modeling	Linear performance pricing

Demand power

About the authors

Alenka Triplat is a member of A.T. Kearney 's Operations Practice. In five years with the firm in Vienna, Austria, she has carried out and led multiple projects on supply management topics in construction equipment, packaging, and steel sectors. She has worked with international clients based in Austria, Germany and Eastern European countries, and spent longer periods of time working and living in the USA. Her areas of expertise include supply management topics, such as US-Dollar-sourcing, negotiation strategies and global sourcing. She is a trainer in sourcing strategies and negotiations and has published multiple articles on these topics. Alenka Triplat studied economics at the University of Ljubljana (Slovenia) and business administration at Vienna University of Economics and Business Administration (Austria). She currently lives in Vienna and Ljubljana.